SPANISH BUSINESS CORRESPONDENCE

In the same series

French Business Correspondence
Stuart Williams and Nathalie McAndrew-Cazorla
German Business Correspondence
Paul Hartley and Gertrud Robins
Italian Business Correspondence
Vincent Edwards and Gianfranca Gessa Shepheard
French Business Situations *
Stuart Williams and Nathalie McAndrew-Cazorla
German Business Situations *
Paul Hartley and Gertrud Robins
Italian Business Situations *
Vincent Edwards and Gianfranca Gessa Shepheard
Spanish Business Situations *
Michael Gorman and María-Luisa Henson
Manual of Business French
Stuart Williams and Nathalie McAndrew-Cazorla
Manual of Business German
Paul Hartley and Gertrud Robins
Manual of Business Italian
Vincent Edwards and Gianfranca Gessa Shepheard
Manual of Business Spanish
Michael Gorman and María-Luisa Henson

*Accompanying cassettes available

SPANISH BUSINESS CORRESPONDENCE

Michael Gorman
and
María-Luisa Henson

London and New York

Michael Gorman and **María-Luisa Henson** are Senior Lecturers in Spanish at the School of Languages and European Studies, University of Wolverhampton.

In the preparation of this handbook every effort was made to avoid the use of actual company names or trade names. If any has been used inadvertently, the publishers will change it in any future reprint if they are notified.

First published 1996
by Routledge
2 Park Square, Milton Park, Abingdon, Oxon, OX14 4RN

Simultaneously published in the USA and Canada
by Routledge
270 Madison Ave, New York NY 10016

Transferred to Digital Printing 2005

© 1996 Michael Gorman and María-Luisa Henson

Typeset in Rockwell and Univers by Solidus (Bristol) Ltd

British Library Cataloguing in Publication Data
A catalogue record for this book is available from the British Library

Library of Congress Cataloguing in Publication Data
Gorman, Michael, 1944–
    Spanish business correspondence/Michael Gorman and María-Luisa Henson.
        p. cm. – (Languages for business)
    English and Spanish.
    1. Commercial correspondence, Spanish. I. Henson, María-Luisa.
    II. Title. III. Series.
HF5728.S7G652 1996
808'.066651061–dc20   96–20559
ISBN 0–415–13713–6

Contents

Spanish commercial correspondence   2
   General notes

1   Enquiry about a product   6
   Solicitando información sobre un producto

2   Enquiry about prices   8
   Solicitando precios

3   Enquiry about a company   10
   Solicitando informes sobre una empresa

4   Enquiry about a person   12
   Solicitando informes personales

5   Enquiry asking for a specific quote   14
   Solicitando presupuesto determinado

6   Soliciting an agency   16
   Ofreciendo servicio de agencia

7   Requesting information about agents   18
   Solicitando información sobre agentes

8   Giving information about agents   20
   Dando información sobre agentes

9   Request for a business reference   22
   Solicitando información sobre un negocio

10   Favourable reply to request for a business reference   24
   Respuesta favorable a la petición de referencias comerciales

11   Unfavourable reply to request for a business reference   26
   Respuesta desfavorable a la petición de referencias comerciales

12   Evasive reply to request for a business reference   28
   Respuesta evasiva a la petición de referencias comerciales

13   Placing an order   30
   Solicitando un pedido

14   Cancellation of order   32
   Anulando un pedido

15   Confirming a telephone order   34
   Confirmando un pedido efectuado por teléfono

16   Making an order for specific items of office equipment   36
   Solicitando un pedido de enseres de oficina

17 Acknowledgement of an order 38
Acusando recibo de un pedido

18 Payment of invoices – Letter accompanying payment 40
Pago de facturas – Carta acompañada de pago

19 Payment of invoices – Request for deferral 42
Pago de facturas – Petición de aplazamiento

20 Payment of invoices – Refusal to pay 44
Pago de facturas – Negándose a efectuar un pago

21 Apologies for non-payment 46
Pidiendo excusas por no efectuar un pago

22 Request for payment 48
Petición de un pago

23 Overdue account – First letter 50
Pago atrasado – Primera notificación

24 Overdue account – Final letter 52
Pago atrasado – Última notificación

25 Job advertisement – Letter to newspaper 54
Anuncio de puesto de trabajo – Carta a revista

26 Job advertisement 56
Anuncio de puesto de trabajo

27 Asking for further details and application form 58
Pidiendo información e impreso de solicitud para un puesto de trabajo

28 Job application 60
Solicitud de empleo

29 Curriculum vitae 62
Curriculum vitae

30 Unsolicited letter of application 64
Solicitando empleo no anunciado

31 Interview invitation 66
Llamada a una entrevista

32 Favourable reply to job application 68
Respuesta favorable a una solicitud de empleo

33 Unfavourable reply to job application 70
Respuesta desfavorable a una solicitud de empleo

34 Requesting a reference for a job applicant 72
Pidiendo referencias sobre una persona que solicita un puesto de trabajo

35 Providing a positive reference for an employee 74
Respuesta favorable a una petición de referencias

36 Acceptance letter   76
    Aceptando un puesto de trabajo

37 Contract of employment   78
    Contrato de trabajo

38 Enquiring about regulations for purchase of property abroad   82
    (memo)
    Pidiendo información sobre adquisición immobiliaria en el
    extranjero (comunicado interno)

39 Advising of delay in delivery (telex)   84
    Notificando el retraso de una entrega (télex)

40 Seeking clarification of financial position (fax)   86
    Solicitando aclaración sobre situación financiera (fax)

41 Reporting to client on availability of particular property (fax)   88
    Informando a un cliente sobre disponibilidad de una determinada
    propiedad (fax)

42 Complaining about customs delay (fax)   90
    Quejándose por el retraso en la Aduana (fax)

43 Stating delivery conditions   92
    Confirmando condiciones de entrega

44 Confirming time/place of delivery   94
    Confirmando hora y lugar de entrega

45 Checking on mode of transportation   96
    Comprobando modo de transporte

46 Claiming for transportation damage   98
    Reclamando daños de transporte

47 Enquiring about customs clearance   100
    Pidiendo información sobre mercancías pendientes de despacho
    en Aduana

48 Undertaking customs formalities   102
    Emprendiendo formalidades aduaneras

49 Informing of storage facilities   104
    Informando sobre facilidades de almacenamiento

50 Assuring of confidentiality of information   106
    Asegurando confidencialidad en la información

51 Informing a client on conditions of loans/mortgages available   108
    Informando a un cliente sobre condiciones de préstamo/créditos
    hipotecarios

52 Circulating local businesses with property services available   110
    Difundiendo información a empresas locales sobre servicios
    inmobiliarios

53 Advertising maintenance services available for office equipment   112
    Anunciando servicios de mantenimiento para equipos de oficina

54 Arranging a meeting for further discussions   114
    Concertando una reunión para tratar de un tema con más detalle

55 Reservations – Enquiry about hotel accommodation (fax)   116
    Reservas – Pidiendo información sobre alojamiento en un hotel (fax)

56 Reservations – Confirmation of reservation (fax)   118
    Reservas – Confirmando una reserva (fax)

57 Reservations – Change of arrival date   120
    Reservas – Cambio de la llegada al hotel

58 Reservations – Request for confirmation of reservation   122
    Reservas – Pidiendo información sobre confirmación de una reserva

59 Insurance – Request for quotation for fleet car insurance   124
    Seguro – Solicitando presupuesto para asegurar flota de vehículos

60 Insurance – Reminder of overdue premium   126
    Seguro – Aviso de vencimiento de prima

61 Insurance – Submission of documents to support claim   128
    Seguro – Presentando documentos para apoyar una reclamación

62 Insurance – Taking out third party vehicle insurance   130
    Seguro – Seguro de vehículo a terceros

63 Insurance – Refusal to meet claim   132
    Seguro – Negándose a saldar un reclamo

64 Considering legal action   134
    Asesoramiento legal: daños

65 Requesting information on setting up a plant abroad   136
    Asesoramiento legal: compra de bienes en el extranjero

66 Complaint about delay in administering a bank account   138
    Queja sobre demora en la gestión de una cuenta bancaria

67 Complaint about mail delivery   140
    Queja sobre reparto de correo

68 Complaint about wrong consignment of goods   142
    Queja sobre entrega errónea de mercancías

69 Complaint about damage to goods   144
    Queja sobre artículos dañados

70 Informing customers that a company has been taken over   146
    Informando sobre cambios en una empresa: adquisición

71 Informing customers of change of name and address   148
    Informando sobre cambio de nombre y dirección de una empresa

72 Informing customers of increased prices 150
Informando sobre cambios de precios

73 Requesting information about opening a business account 152
*Solicitando información sobre la apertura de cuenta bancaria de
negocios*

74 Requesting information about opening a personal bank account 154
Solicitando información sobre apertura de cuenta corriente

75 Letter re overdrawn account 156
Carta en relación con estado de cuenta en números rojos

76 Informing a customer of a bank deposit 158
Notificando al cliente sobre transferencia a su favor

77 Enquiry about banking – Letter from the Ombudsman 160
Solicitando información sobre la banca – Carta del Defensor

78 Enquiry about post office banking facilities 162
Correos: solicitando información sobre operaciones bancarias

79 Enquiry about opening a post office account 164
Solicitando información sobre apertura de cuenta por giro postal

80 Opening poste restante 166
Retención de correspondencia en lista

Business Correspondence

Spanish commercial correspondence – general notes

The business letter in Spanish is subject to certain conventions in respect of its layout, its language register and its contents. There are also differences between practice in Spain and in the many Spanish-speaking countries of Latin America. Apart from a tendency in the latter area to continue with expressions or formulae now regarded as rather outmoded in Spain itself, there is naturally an American influence in commercial correspondence and it should be noted that there are minor variations in practice between individual countries. However, by observing what is current practice in Spain (and here too there is an increasing flexibility due to influence from EU nations and the USA), writers and readers of business correspondence should not experience difficulty in dealing with Latin American contacts.

Style of letter-writing

First, it must be said that spoken registers rarely appear in such correspondence, as is also the case elsewhere in the world; second, the phenomenon of 'formality' in Spanish-language expression is established primarily via the use of *usted/ustedes* (as opposed to *tú/vosotros*) and thereafter by the use of certain syntactic mechanisms, verb forms and lexical items. For example, subject pronouns referring directly to those involved in the transaction are avoided, the impersonal *se* expressions (with third person verb forms) frequently replacing them; the use of first person plural verbs and pronouns, as opposed to the singular, suggests corporate responsibility (and therefore more *gravitas*); the use of the complicated subjunctive mood is very widespread in business correspondence; a more abstract and perhaps lengthier item of vocabulary will appear even where there is a quite acceptable alternative. Sentence structure can therefore sometimes be lengthy and dense, conveying at best a necessary gravity or respect for detail, and at worst pomposity or obscurity. Equally, there are business letters that reduce their message and length almost to a telex format.

Company names

Most Spanish companies use stationery with a printed letterhead (*el membrete*) which includes its logo, name, address and telephone number; fax, telex and VAT numbers may also appear here. The name of the company is frequently followed by the letters S.A. (*Sociedad Anónima*), which indicate that it is an entity closely resembling a plc. These letters are sometimes incorporated into the company's name (e.g. Enfisa, Matesa); other cases, usually smaller companies, are S.L. or S.R.L. (*Sociedad de Responsabilidad Limitada*), *y Co* or *y Cía* ('and Company'), *e hijos/y hermanos* ('and sons/brothers'). In the *membrete*, or more likely at the foot of the company stationery, may appear the names of the directors, branch addresses and the company's official registered number. The main company information might appear at the top left of the page rather than in the top centre part of it.

Letter layout

Explained schematically, the rest of the letter would be as follows if observing the conventions (not necessarily the norm):

Left-hand side of page

Your Reference (*Su Referencia*): letters or numbers etc.
Our Reference (*Nuestra Referencia*): letters or numbers etc.
(The main terms might be printed on the stationery and might appear in reverse order from the one above.) Equally this information might appear below the address of the recipient.

The date:	Place	–	Day	–	of	–	Month	–	of	–	Year
e.g.	Almería		11		de		mayo		de		199-

The date can also appear on the right-hand side of the page, well above the body of the text. The place of origin is sometimes omitted if it is obvious from the *membrete*; the actual date details are sometimes reduced to figures only.

The name and address of the person/company to receive the letter (also known as the 'inside address') is allotted one line per item:

- Title (*Sr/Sra/Srta/Dr*) + first name/initials + surname(s)
- Role in company
- Company name
- Street/road name followed by numbers of building and floor
- City/town name (plus code)
- Province (plus code)
- Country

The post code for each town is added to the province number (a specific number between 1 and 50), thus invariably making a five-digit full code. To phone a Spanish town from outside Spain you dial 00 + 34 + the provincial code (*minus* its initial 9) shown in international directories + the subscriber's number.

A letter can be directed to a specified person by placing below the address a statement to the effect: *Para/A la atención de . . .*; similarly, the precise purpose of the letter can be noted on the next line as follows: *Asunto . . . .* If the contents of the letter are confidential, either/both *Privado* and *Confidencial* would appear after the inside address.

Opening lines

When addressing a known person, the following salutation is customary: *Estimado Sr* + surname/*Estimada Sra* + surname. First names can be included here, but not in the form of initials. If the person is not known (and therefore the

3

letter is probably addressed to the company in general, to a department, or to an unnamed Head of . . .) it is customary to use the more generic salutation: *Muy señor mío* ('Dear Sir')/*Muy señora mía* ('Dear Madam'). Plurals can also be used here (e.g. *Muy señores míos/Muy señoras nuestras*), suggesting a broader approach on either side. Note that it is preferable to maintain singular or plural reference, according to the salutation, throughout a given item of correspondence; in practice, however, the two are at times mixed.

Plain *Señor(es)* is frequently used to greet the unknown addressee(s), as it allows for virtually any nuance of interpretation. A letter might also be directed to *Señor/Sr Director* or *Señora/Sra Secretaria* as an unknown postholder, and when first names are included to a known person it is still possible to use the traditional title *Don/Doña* (e.g. *Sr Don Miguel Valdés*). There are several other, more official, titles available in Spanish (e.g. *Presidente, Doctora, Excelencia*), but these of course are used only in very specific contexts. Note also that after the opening salutation in Spanish a colon, as opposed to the English comma, is used (e.g. *Estimada Sra Ruiz:*).

Style

The format of most business letters in Spanish is now blocked to the left, with the opening paragraph sometimes commencing in line with the end of the salutation. This is the only systematic style occurring in the text (see examples of letters in main section). There is also a tendency to allow a wider horizontal gap between the salutation and the main body of the letter. Capital letters are not as commonly used in Spanish as in English; their use in certain abbreviations (e.g. *Vd., Sra*) has already been noted, and they appear also where a specific person, rather than just a role or title, is alluded to (e.g. *el Presidente, el Jefe de Ventas, la Directora*). However, as a sign of courtesy in a business letter, certain positions like those above may be accorded *mayúscula* (capital letter) status even where no specific individual is concerned. When accompanied by the name of a person, all titles are capitalized if that person is being addressed; proper nouns for companies, people, places, products etc., are naturally accorded initial capitals. Spelling is relatively easy in Spanish as the language is phonetic. Thus, although the appropriate register/tone for commercial correspondence requires careful cultivation, imitating the style of authentic sources is a sensible way of achieving the impersonal, courteous (and frequently euphemistic) mode of expression characteristic of most Spanish business correspondence.

Closing lines

Just as in English and other languages, the 'complimentary close' (*la despedida*) is essential; a range of typical endings is shown in the main letters section, and many are interchangeable. Clearly, however, it is important to ensure that there is a degree of compatibility between the salutation and the close. As a rule the use of *Estimado/a* in the initial greeting permits use of the adverb *cordialmente* at the close, whilst *Muy señor/a mío/a* suggests *atentamente* for the close. The basic verb used in this part of the letter is *saludar*, and invariably the writer expresses his/her greeting as a third person (*saluda*), thereby confirming the element of formality. In recent times a whole variety of expressions has emerged in both formal and informal correspondence.

Beneath the *despedida* the writer signs his/her name and the following typed version of the name usually mirrors exactly the signature, which may include initials for the first name(s) and one or both surnames, depending upon the preferences of the writer. Below this name usually appears the role or position in the organization of the sender (e.g. *Encargada de Márketing*, *Jefe de Personal*, *Director Gerente*). If the letter is signed on behalf of somebody else (p.p.) the inscription *p/o* (*por orden*) appears beside the typed name. Any copies of the letter sent to others are indicated, as in English, by c.c. at the foot of the page. Similarly, enclosures (*anexos*) in the envelope are indicated by the appearance of that word near the left margin below all other information in the letter; the word *adjunto* may also be used to indicate that there are accompanying enclosures.

Envelopes

The envelope (*el sobre*) is normally filled out exactly as the details of the addressee appear in the letter itself, and the front of the envelope may bear any one of a number of inscriptions to identify to the postal service or to the recipients the nature of the missive (e.g. *urgente*, *por avión*, *confidencial*, *a reexpedir*, *impresos*). The back flap of the envelope normally bears the surname and address of the sender (*remitente*) after the latter word itself, or *remite*, or *Rte*.

Note on translations

The documents presented here in parallel text are not a word-for-word translation of each other. Due to obvious differences in letter-writing style in Spain (and Latin America) and the business vocabulary used, it is only possible to offer an approximate version of the Spanish letter in the English text particularly in respect of names, figures, etc.

1 Enquiry about a product

4 January 199-

Augustin SA
Z.I. de l'Empereur
F-19200 Ussel
France

Dear Sir/Madam

RE: TOOTHPICK MAKING & PACKAGING MACHINE

We represent a major distributor of foodstuffs and other related materials in Kenya.

We have found your name in *Kompass* under the category of suppliers of toothpick-making machinery. Our present requirement is for a special toothpick-making and packaging machine. If you do produce such equipment or can supply it we would be pleased to receive your earliest quotation CIF Mombasa, prices for this machine and its equipment, together with a stated delivery time.

Please would you also quote for the installation of this machine in the Ususu factory in Mombasa.

We look forward to your earliest reply and remain

Yours faithfully

John Mason
Technical Director

1 Solicitando información sobre un producto

Hnos.[1] Godoy
Polígono[2] Nuevo, Unidad 45
Palencia,[3] ESPAÑA.   4 de enero de 199-

Asunto: Máquina de fabricación y envasadora de palillos

Estimado/a Sr/Sra:[4]

Representamos a un importante distribuidor de comestibles y otras materias relacionadas con esta industria en Kenia.

Su nombre figuraba en *Kompass* bajo la denominación de abastecedores de maquinaria de fabricación de palillos. Necesitamos disponer de una máquina especial al objeto de fabricar y envasar palillos. Si usted[5] es fabricante de dicha maquinaria, o la abastece, le agradeceríamos nos enviara[6] lo antes posible presupuesto CIF[7] Mombasa, precios de esta máquina y material complementario, junto con la fecha de entrega.

Asimismo, sírvase[8] comunicarnos precio de instalación de la misma[9] en nuestra fábrica de Ususu, en Mombasa.

En espera de una pronta contestación, le saludamos[10] muy atentamente.

Gianni Mussini
Director Técnico

1 Abbreviation of *Hermanos* ('brothers').
2 *Polígono*: industrial/trading estate typical of economic development in Spain since the 1960s.
3 The Spanish town/city name is frequently preceded here by a five-digit code; the first two digits refer to its province.
4 Abbreviation for *Señor/Señora* ('Mr'/'Mrs') – also *Señorita* ('Ms') abbreviated to *Srta* – is normal here. *Estimado/a*: the most simple, and increasingly popular, of several virtually equivalent ways of greeting the addressee.
5 *Usted* (abbreviated to *Vd.*): formal mode of 'you' singular form of address, used with third person verbs and pronouns. In Latin America *usted* is yet more widespread; its plural (*ustedes*) is used in Latin America for any 'you' plural; whilst in Spain *vosotros* (plural of *tú*: informal) is also used, informally. *Tú* and *vosotros* would not be used in commercial correspondence.
6 Conditional tense followed by imperfect subjunctive: a complex verb structure typical of Spanish commercial correspondence.
7 CIF: English abbreviation used in Spanish, whose equivalent is *coste* ('cost'), *seguro* ('insurance'), *flete* ('freight').
8 One of several ways to say 'please' formally.
9 *La misma*: 'the aforementioned', referring back to *máquina*.
10 Plural verb ('we greet') to refer to all in firm enquiring.

2 Enquiry about prices

28 February 199-

Bandani Detergenti SpA
Via A. Lamarmora 75
20093 COLOGNO MONZESE (MI)
Italy

Dear Sir/Madam

RE: QUOTATION RMS 34/16 JAN 199-/TOILET CLEANSER

On 16 January we received a quotation from your company for the supply of
4,000 litres of industrial toilet cleanser and disinfectant. We were unable to justify
ordering this at the time, because we had sufficient stocks from our previous
order at the end of last year.

We would like to enquire now if the prices quoted at the time are still valid for this
commodity.

If you are unequivocally able to confirm that this is the case, please take this letter
as an order for a further 10,000 litres. If there has been any price increase, please
be so kind as to fax this to us or phone the undersigned, so that we can proceed
and agree a price in due course.

Yours faithfully

Dick DeZwart
Buyer

2 Solicitando precios

Bandani Detergenti s.p.a.
Via A. Lamarmora 75
20093 Cologno Monzese
Milano, ITALIA.   28.2.199-

Asunto: Presupuesto RMS 34/16 enero 199-/detergente limpieza sanitarios[1]

Muy Sr/Sra nuestro/a:[2]

El pasado 16 de enero recibimos de su empresa un
presupuesto para el suministro de 4.000[3] litros de detergente y desinfectante
industrial para la limpieza de sanitarios. Por entonces nos fue imposible aceptar
su oferta ya que disponíamos de suficientes existencias restantes de nuestro
pedido anterior, efectuado a finales del año pasado.

Ahora nos gustaría informarnos si los precios vigentes en aquellas fechas[4] son
todavía válidos para este producto.

Si usted puede confirmarnos, sin dejar lugar a dudas, que esto es así, sírvase
considerar esta carta como un pedido de 10.000 litros más. Si ha habido subida
de precios, tenga a bien enviarnos los precios por fax, o llame al abajo firmante
por teléfono, y así poder proceder y llegar a un acuerdo sobre el precio en su
debido momento.

Reciba[5] atentos saludos.

                                                                    F. Redondo
                                                                    Jefe de Compras

1 Abbreviated format for presentation of main data.
2 A traditional and formal mode of introduction in commercial correspondence (also
   mío/mía): 'Our'/'My Dear Sir'/'Madam'.
3 In Spain a point is used to separate parts of a number over a thousand from one another;
   commas are used to indicate decimal places. In some Latin American countries the
   English system of points and commas is used.
4 Literally, 'on those dates'.
5 The *usted* command form of *recibir*, used with a plural object.

3 Enquiry about a company

7 March 199-

GiardinPrati SpA
Via Cassia Km 89
Val di Paglia
53040 RADICOFANI
Siena
Italy

Dear Sir/Madam

RE: ORDER LAWN-IND/CZ28

We refer to your quotation for 30 industrial mowing machines, model CZ28.

We gather that our client is now eager to proceed with finalizing the order for this equipment as we are slowly approaching spring time. As we have never placed an order with your company, we would like to receive your full audited accounts for the last four trading years.

Please ensure that the above accounts reach us within the next five working days, as we are eager not to miss the six-week delivery time which will enable us to have the equipment in our hands as soon as possible.

Yours faithfully

Lawrence Raines
Sales Department

3 Solicitando informes sobre una empresa

GiardinPrati s.p.a.
Via Cassia Km 89
Val di Paglia
53040 Radicofani
Siena
Italia.   7.3.199-

Asunto: pedido segadora[1] IND/CZ28

Estimado/a Sr/Sra:

Hacemos referencia a su presupuesto para 30 segadoras industriales, modelo CZ28.

Le comunicamos[2] que nuestro cliente está impaciente por pasar a concluir el pedido de esta maquinaria ya que estamos aproximándonos a la primavera. Puesto que nunca hemos hecho ningún pedido a su empresa, nos gustaría recibir de la misma[3] una completa auditoría de los últimos cuatro años de ejercicio.[4]

Le rogamos que dicha auditoría nos llegue[5] en el plazo de los próximos cinco días laborables, ya que no deseamos perder las seis semanas correspondientes al período de entrega que nos permitirían tener la maquinaria en nuestro poder lo antes posible.

Atentamente le saluda,

Lorenzo Ranura
Encargado de Ventas

1 Full word for farm mower, harvester.
2 Included here in Spanish to enhance authenticity.
3 *La misma*: literally, 'the same', referring back to *empresa*.
4 *Ejercicio*: here meaning 'financial year'.
5 Present subjunctive after *Le rogamos que . . .*

4 Enquiry about a person

11 September 199-

ROPER Industriale
Viale San Benedetto 39–43
20084 Lacchiarella
Milano

Dear Sirs

RE: MR SAMUEL SMITH

We write to you as a fellow producer of machine tools. We have recently received an application from Mr Samuel Smith of Reading (England) who is applying for a post as technical support engineer with our company. This gentleman has given your company's name both as a previous employer and as a character referee.

From our reading of Mr Smith's CV he would appear most suitable for the post. However, we are also keen that people should fit into our factory and we are most concerned that in his early twenties Mr Smith was a very active member of the European Pro-Whale Organization. We would appreciate your comments on this, as we are keen to be better informed about this candidate.

Yours faithfully

Carlo Ruggeri
Personnel Manager

4 Solicitando informes personales

Roper Industries
Polywide Science Park
Basingstoke
Hampshire
Inglaterra.   11.9.199-

Asunto: El[1] Sr Samuel Smith

Señores:

     Nos ponemos en contacto con ustedes como cofabricantes[2] de
máquinas herramienta. Ultimamente hemos recibido una solicitud del Sr Samuel
Smith, de Reading, en la que nos solicita un puesto como ayudante de ingeniero
técnico. Dicho señor nos ha proporcionado el nombre de su empresa para poder
pedirle referencias personales y profesionales del mismo ya que fue empleado
suyo.[3]

A juzgar por su currículum vitae, el Sr Smith parece ser el candidato idóneo. No
obstante, tenemos mucho interés en que nuestros futuros empleados se ajusten
a nuestra fábrica, y nos preocupa el hecho de que cuando el Sr Smith era
veinteañero fuera un miembro muy activo de la Organización Europea en favor
de las Ballenas. Les agradeceríamos nos hicieran las pertinentes observaciones
acerca de este asunto, ya que tenemos mucho interés en obtener información
más amplia de este candidato.[4]

Les saluda atte.[5]

                                           Carlos Rivera Sanz
                                        Director de Personal

1 The article *El/el* (or *La/la*) is included before a person's surname when talking **about**
    him/her, as opposed to **to** him/her. In abbreviated form (*Sr* for *Señor, Sra* for *Señora,*
    Srta for *Señorita*) the capital *S* of the title (equivalent to 'Mr'/'Mrs'/'Ms') is invariably
    retained. Where the full title is used, other than at the beginning of a sentence, the
    tendency is to write the initial in lower case (e.g. *La señorita Gómez*).
2 *Cofabricantes* implies joint activity; *fabricante homólogo* would imply only equivalent
    activity.
3 A paraphrase in Spanish for enhanced authenticity of expression.
4 Alternative, for most general use: *aspirante.*
5 Common abbreviation of *atentamente.*

5 Enquiry asking for a specific quote

2 April 199-

Sales Manager
OFFICE 2000
89–91 Scott Road
Olton
Solihull
West Midlands
B92 7RZ

Dear Sir/Madam

RE: LASER PHOTOCOPIER PR3000

We have been in correspondence with your company over the last six months and have in that time received a number of different quotations for different models of the industrial laser photocopying machines produced by your company. We have decided that the most suitable machine for our requirement is the PR3000.

We note, however, that your price of £4,000 is for one machine only. We are keen to purchase 20 printers of this particular model and we would therefore like to know what your discount would be on an order of this magnitude.

We would also like to know the delivery time for this equipment. If it were possible to deliver the printers in two separate batches of 10 each, we would require the first delivery in three months' time and the second some two months after that, when our new British office is completed in Cromer.

Yours faithfully

Luca Evangelista
Sales Manager

5 Solicitando presupuesto determinado

Director de Ventas, Office 2000
89–91 Scott Road
Olton, Solihull
West Midlands B92 7RZ
Inglaterra.   2.4.199-

Asunto: Fotocopiadora láser PR3000

Estimado/a Sr/Sra:

   Llevamos unos seis meses manteniendo correspondencia con
su empresa, y durante ese tiempo hemos recibido diversas cotizaciones para
diferentes modelos de máquinas fotocopiadoras láser, tipo industrial, fabricadas
por su empresa. Hemos acordado que la más apropiada a nuestros requisitos es
la PR3000.

Sin embargo, observamos que el precio de 4.000 libras esterlinas que nos dieron
se refería sólo al de una máquina. Deseamos comprar veinte impresoras[1] de este
determinado modelo y, por lo tanto, nos gustaría saber cuál sería[2] el descuento
en un pedido de esta magnitud.

Nos gustaría saber, asimismo, la fecha de entrega de dicho equipo. Si hubiera
posibilidad de entregar las impresoras en dos partidas distintas de diez envíos[3]
en cada una, necesitaríamos la primera dentro de tres meses, y la segunda unos
dos meses después, cuando esté[4] terminada nuestra nueva oficina ubicada en
Cromer, Inglaterra.

Le saluda cordialmente.

              Luis Evangelista
             Director de Ventas

1 *Impresoras* is used here to refer to the copiers; it is also the generic term for 'computer
 printer'.
2 Accent on *cuál* indicates indirect question; conditional *sería* emphasizes speculation on
 this deal rather than usual discount.
3 Here *envíos* implies the ten individual machines to be sent.
4 Present subjunctive *esté* to indicate indefinite future time.

6 Soliciting an agency

4 December 199-

Erwin Page plc
Electrical Appliances & Supplies
29 Landon Place
London
SE45 9AS

Dear Sirs

We have heard from business associates that you are looking for an agency for the promotion of your products in the US. We feel therefore that we may be of assistance to you: we are a long established agency with offices in the midwest and on the west coast of the United States, and are experienced in the sale and promotion of domestic electrical equipment. We have helped several British firms to boost their US sales, and are convinced that you too could benefit from our experience. Our UK representative, Charles J Parker, would be pleased to call on you to discuss your needs further: you can contact him on 0171 745 4756. In any event Mr Parker will be visiting your locality in the coming week, and will take the opportunity of calling on you.

Yours faithfully

Peter Bowles
Director

6 Ofreciendo servicio de agencia

Ernesto Valderrama e hijos
Paseo de la Paz, 34
Quito
Ecuador.   4.12.199-

Muy señores nuestros:

De acuerdo con lo que nos han comunicado nuestros socios, ustedes buscan una agencia que se encargue[1] de la promoción de sus productos en los Estados Unidos. Por lo tanto, pensamos que nosotros podríamos serles de utilidad: nuestra agencia lleva muchos años establecida, y tenemos oficinas en la zona central de EE.UU. así como en la costa oeste del país. Tenemos experiencia considerable en la venta y promoción de electrodomésticos. Hemos ayudado a varias empresas sudamericanas a estimular sus ventas en los Estados Unidos, y estamos convencidos de que ustedes podrían beneficiarse también de nuestra experiencia. Nuestro representante en su país, Charles J. Parker, estará gustoso en hacerles una visita para tratar con más detalle sus necesidades: pueden ponerse en contacto con él llamando al 2 45475. En todo caso, el Sr Parker visitará su localidad la semana próxima, y aprovechará la ocasión para visitarles.

Sin otro particular,[2] les saluda cordialmente,

Peter Bowles
(Socio mayoritario)

1 Verb in the subjunctive because the *agencia* mentioned is (only) hypothetical at this
   stage.
2 A standard expression to end a business letter: 'with no more to add'.

7 Requesting information about agents

23 July 199-

Duperrier SA
24 avenue des Sylphides
Brignoles
83170 Var
France

Dear Sirs

RE: LÜTTICH GmbH

We have heard from colleagues that you have recently used the services of
Lüttich GmbH as agents for your products in Germany. We are in a different line
of business from yourselves, but we believe that Lüttich represents companies of
various kinds. We are looking for agents in Germany and Switzerland for our
stationery products. We should be grateful if you could let us have further
information on the above-named firm. Any information you send us will be
treated with the strictest confidence.

Yours faithfully

P Brandauer
Sales Department

7 Solicitando información sobre agentes

Duperrier S.A.
24 avenue des Sylphides
Brignoles
83170 Var
Francia.   23.7.199-

Asunto: Lüttich GmbH

Señores:

Hemos sabido por unos colegas que recientemente ustedes se sirvieron[1]
de Lüttich GmbH como representantes de sus productos en Alemania. Nosotros
llevamos un negocio distinto al suyo,[2] pero nos consta que Lüttich representa a
empresas de varios tipos. Buscamos agentes comerciales que representen
nuestros productos de papelería en Alemania y Suiza. Les agradecería nos
proporcionaran más información de la empresa arriba mencionada. Toda
información[3] será tratada confidencialmente.

Atentamente les saluda.[4]

                                          Pablo Banderilla
                                          (Depto. de Ventas)

1 *Servirse de*: 'to use', 'to make use of'.
2 *Suyo* (*de usted*): 'yours'.
3 Implies 'information you send us'.
4 This final greeting can end variably: with a comma, a full stop, or nothing before the
   signature in Spanish-language correspondence.

8 Giving information about agents

8 August 199-

Herrn H Pike
Heinrich Pittmann GmbH
Ofterdingenstraße 69
6800 Mannheim
Germany

Dear Mr Pike

RE: DIETER & HELLER

Thank you for your letter enquiring about the company Dieter and Heller, who have been agents for our products for several years. This company has represented our interests in Eastern and Central Europe very effectively and our sales in those regions have been buoyant as a result. You will find their Bonn-based manager, Max Lettmann, particularly helpful, and I am sure he will be interested in co-operating with you.

If you do contact him, don't hesitate to mention my name.

Yours sincerely

Maria Fischer

8 Dando información sobre agentes

Sr R. Caminero
Farmacéuticos Ledesma S.A.
Carretera del Norte
Oviedo
España.   8.8.199-

Asunto: Dieter y Heller

Estimado Sr Caminero:

       Le agradezco[1] su carta en la que pide información sobre la empresa Dieter y Heller, con la cual llevamos varios años trabajando en la promoción de nuestros productos. Dicha empresa nos ha representado eficazmente en la Europa Central y del Este, y como resultado las ventas de nuestros productos en esas áreas han sido de demanda intensiva.[2] El Sr Max Lettmann, director en Bonn, le será muy útil, y estoy segura que estará muy interesado en cooperar con usted.

Si contacta con él, podrá mencionarle mi nombre con toda confianza.

Le saluda atentamente

                                   Maria Fischer

1 First person verb, 'I thank'; note third person form in final greeting.
2 More literally, 'in great demand'.

9 Request for a business reference

11 March 199-

<u>CONFIDENTIAL</u>

Mr G Le Blanc
Sales Director
CURTAINS & BLINDS Ltd
PO Box 181
Croydon
CR0 5SN

Dear Mr Le Blanc

<u>RE: CASELLACCI SpA</u>

We would like to introduce our company as a major supplier of castors for office furniture. We have been approached by Casellacci SPA of Pisa as potential distributors of our products in the Italian market. Mr Casellacci has explained that he has been supplying your range of curtain fittings in the market for some fifteen years and has a proven track record of both successful sales and prompt payment with your company.

We are eager to proceed in the Italian market, but we wish to have some reassurance about this company, as we do not know either the company or the individuals concerned. It would appear that they are selling only high quality products and that our range of castors would fit very well into their sales range.

We would appreciate your earliest comments and thank you in advance for providing this information, which we would treat in the utmost confidence.

Yours sincerely

Steve Watwood
Export Manager

9 Solicitando información sobre un negocio

Sr G. Blanco
Director de Ventas
Cortinas y Persianas Luján
Avenida Elche, 34
Valencia
España.   11 de marzo de 199-

Asunto: Casellacci s.p.a. (Confidencial)

Estimado Sr Blanco:

Nos gustaría presentarle a nuestra empresa[1] como importante abastecedora de ruedecillas para mobiliario de oficina. Casellacci s.p.a. de Pisa se ha dirigido a nosotros para actuar como posibles distribuidores de nuestros productos en el mercado italiano. El Sr Casellacci nos ha explicado que él lleva aproximadamente quince años suministrando su gama de accesorios de cortinas, y que tiene antecedentes garantizados en el éxito de las ventas y el pago rápido con su empresa.

Estamos deseosos de introducirnos en el mercado italiano, pero queremos estar completamente seguros acerca de esta empresa ya que no conocemos a la susodicha[2] ni a sus empleados. Parece ser que sólo se dedican a la venta de productos de alta calidad y que nuestra gama de ruedecillas se ajustaría perfectamente a la suya.[3]

A este respecto,[4] le agradeceríamos su pronto comentario y le damos las gracias anticipadas por esta información que guardaríamos estrictamente confidencial.

Quedo atento y seguro servidor[5] de usted.

Steve Watwood
Director de Exportación

---

1 Alternatives for *empresa*: *compañía, firma, entidad, casa*.
2 *La susodicha*: 'the abovementioned' (company).
3 *La suya*: 'theirs' (i.e. their range – *gama* – of castors).
4 'In this regard'.
5 Note first person verb and use of *servidor*: 'I remain your . . . servant'.

10 Favourable reply to request for a business reference

23 March 199-

Mr S Watwood
Castassist
158–161 Cressex Estate
New Malden
Surrey
KT13 4EY

Dear Mr Watwood

RE: CASELLACCI SpA OF PISA

We thank you for your letter of 11 March, regarding the company Casellacci of Italy as potential distributors of your range of castors.

We have indeed been working with Casellacci now for 23 years and know both Andrea Casellacci and his son Antonio, who has become more active in the company over the last few years. Casellacci have a number of most competent sales personnel covering the whole of Italy and the islands and have performed most effectively for our company against our large German competitors within the market. Casellacci have over this period of time proven to be most prompt in their payment. At the time of writing I cannot recall any undue delay in the company's settlement of their bills.

I have some knowledge of your company and its products and I am quite sure they are suited to the Italian market. I trust that the Casellacci company will prove a dependable and successful distributor for your product.

We hope you find this information sufficient to your requirements. Should you need any further comments please do not hesitate to contact us.

Yours sincerely

George Le Blanc
Sales Director

10 Respuesta favorable a la petición de referencias comerciales

Sr S Watwood,
Castassist
158–161 Cressex Estate
New Malden
Surrey
KT13 4EY
INGLATERRA.   23.3.199-

Asunto: Casellacci s.p.a. de Pisa

Estimado Sr Watwood:

Le agradecemos su atta. carta del 11 de marzo, en la que nos hace referencia a la empresa Casellacci de Italia como posibles distribuidores de su gama de ruedecillas.

Por supuesto[1] que llevamos trabajando con Casellacci desde hace[2] ahora veintititrés años y conocemos a Andrea Casellacci y a su hijo Antonio, el cual juega un papel más importante en la empresa desde hace unos años.

Casellacci cuenta con un personal de ventas muy competente que se extiende por toda Italia y las islas,[3] y ha llevado a cabo una labor muy provechosa para nuestra empresa frente a nuestros grandes competidores alemanes en el mercado. Casellacci ha demostrado ser durante este período de tiempo muy puntual en efectuar sus pagos. En el momento de escribir la presente,[4] no recuerdo que la mencionada empresa se haya retrasado en la liquidación de sus facturas nunca.

Tengo conocimiento de su empresa de usted y sus productos, y estoy plenamente[5] seguro que se adaptarán bien al mercado italiano. Confío en que la firma Casellacci tendrá seriedad y éxito como distribuidora de su producto.

Esperamos que esta información sea suficiente. En caso de requerir más detalles, no dude[6] en contactarnos.

Le saluda atentamente.

Gerardo Blanco
Director de Ventas

1 Literally, 'of course'.
2 *Desde hace*: literally, 'since ago', used with present tense.
3 Referring mainly to Sardinia and Sicily.
4 *La presente* (i.e. *carta*): 'letter'.
5 Literally, 'fully'.
6 Negative formal command: 'don't doubt/hesitate to . . .'.

11 Unfavourable reply to request for a business reference

23 March 199-

Mr S Watwood
Castassist
158–161 Cressex Estate
New Malden
Surrey
KT13 4EY

Dear Mr Watwood

RE: CASELLACCI SpA OF PISA

We are in receipt of your letter regarding the company of Andrea Casellacci with whom you have been discussing the potential distribution of your products in the Italian market.

We must first ask you to accept our comments on this company in the most confidential terms. We have indeed been working with Casellacci for many years, but unfortunately six months ago Mr Andrea Casellacci was detained by the Italian police and due to this certain irregularities within the company have come to light. A direct result of this situation, in our particular case, is that we have not received payment for the last three major shipments of goods to Casellacci, which were due to us at different times. We are at the moment in discussions with our solicitors who will be undertaking the appropriate action on our behalf.

As a result of this, it is our opinion that although this company has performed successfully in the past, it is obviously not in a position to continue this work on our behalf and therefore we would advise you that it would not be a suitable partner for you at this time.

Yours sincerely

George Le Blanc
Sales Director

11 Respuesta desfavorable a la petición de referencias comerciales

Sr S. Watwood,
Castassist
158–161 Cressex Estate
New Malden
Surrey
KT13 4EY, INGLATERRA.   23.3.199-

Asunto: Casellacci s.p.a. de Pisa

Estimado Sr Watwood:

Obra en nuestro poder[1] su atenta carta en la que nos hace referencia a la empresa de Andrea Casellacci con la que ha tratado sobre la posible distribución de los productos de su empresa de usted en el mercado italiano.

En primer lugar queremos rogarle[2] acepte los comentarios que pasamos a exponerle sobre esta empresa de forma totalmente confidencial. Llevamos[3] trabajando con los Casellacci[4] muchos años, pero por desgracia el Sr Andrea Casellacci fue detenido hace seis meses por la policía italiana, y debido a ello, han sido descubiertas[5] ciertas irregularidades dentro de la empresa. La consecuencia directa de este problema, en nuestro caso, es que no hemos recibido el pago por los tres últimos embarques importantes de mercancías que hemos despachado a Casellacci y que deberían haberse abonado[6] en distintas fechas. Por ahora el asunto está en manos de nuestros abogados, quienes tomarán las medidas necesarias en nombre nuestro.

Por lo tanto, es nuestro criterio que, aunque esta empresa haya[7] tenido éxito en el pasado, queda patente que no está en situación de continuar esta labor en nuestro nombre, y por lo tanto es justo advertirle que, hoy por hoy,[8] no será el socio favorable para usted.

Atentamente le saluda,

Gerardo Blanco
Director de Ventas

1 Literally, 'It acts in our power'.
2 *Rogar*: 'to ask' (formal).
3 For true past perfect meaning: *llevábamos* plus gerund.
4 'The Casellaccis' (i.e. the family).
5 A passive verb construction.
6 *Abonar*: 'to pay' (in, for).
7 *Hubiera* (+ *tenido*) for true past perfect subjunctive.
8 'At present', 'currently'.

27

12 Evasive reply to request for a business reference

23 March 199-

Mr S Watwood
Castassist
158–161 Cressex Estate
New Malden
Surrey
KT13 4EY

Dear Mr Watwood

RE: CASELLACCI SpA OF PISA/ITALY

We are in receipt of your letter regarding the company Casellacci SpA with whom you have been discussing the distribution of your products in the Italian market.

Casellacci are a very reputable company, but we are concerned that they might have already stretched themselves with the selling of our products in Italy. We feel that, if they did take on your range of products, they would probably have to employ a further product manager and perhaps another half a dozen regional sales people to cover the Italian market adequately.

We trust this information is sufficient, but should you require any further comments please do not hesitate to contact us.

Yours sincerely

George Le Blanc
Sales Director

12 Respuesta evasiva a la petición de referencias comerciales

Sr S. Watwood
Castassist
158–161 Cressex Estate
New Malden
Surrey
KT13 4EY
Inglaterra.

23.3.199-

Asunto: Casellacci s.p.a. de Pisa, Italia

Estimado Sr Watwood:

Acusamos recibo[1] de su atta.[2] carta referente a la empresa Casellacci s.p.a. con la que ha estado tratando de la distribución de sus productos de usted en el mercado italiano.

Casellacci es una empresa de muy buena reputación, pero nos preocupa que, tal vez, se hayan sobrepasado con la venta de nuestros productos en Italia; opinamos que si aceptan su gama de productos probablemente tengan que contratar a otro director más de productos y quizás a unos cuantos vendedores regionales más para cubrir debidamente el mercado italiano.

Confiamos en que esta información sea suficiente, pero en caso de no ser así,[3] tengan[4] a bien ponerse en contacto con nosotros.

Cordialmente le saluda,

Gerardo Blanco
Director de Ventas

1 Literally, 'We accuse receipt of . . .' ('we acknowledge').
2 Abbreviation of *atenta*.
3 'If this is not the case . . .': an expansion of the English version.
4 Note frequent and varied use of the subjunctive in this letter. Note also plural form of the verb here even though the letter is addressed to a single person.

13 Placing an order

10 October 199-

Jenkins Freeman plc
Unit 36
Heddington Industrial Estate
Birmingham
B34 9HF

Dear Sirs

We thank you for your catalogue and price list, which we read with interest. On the basis of your current prices, we wish to order the following:

  50 electric drills, model 1456/CB
  50 chain saws, model 1865/CH

Delivery is required by 3.11.199-, and the goods should be delivered to our warehouse in Riddington Way, Battersea. As agreed, payment will be by banker's draft.

Yours faithfully

Gillian Brookes
Purchasing Department

13 Solicitando un pedido

Jiménez y hermanos
Polígono Industrial de Toledo
Toledo
España.   10.10.199-

Señores:

Les damos las gracias[1] por su catálogo y lista de precios que estudiamos con interés. Basándonos en sus precios actuales, procedemos a hacerles el siguiente pedido:

50 taladradoras eléctricas, modelo 1456/CB
50 sierras de cadena, modelo 1865/CH

La entrega ha de[2] efectuarse para el 3.11.199-, y las mercancías deberán ser depositadas en nuestro almacén en Riddington Way, Battersea, Londres. Según acuerdo,[3] el pago deberá efectuarse por giro.

Sin otro particular, les saluda atentamente

Gillian Brookes
Departamento de Compras

1 *Dar las gracias*: a frequent alternative to *agradecer*.
2 *Ha de*: from *haber de*, implying mild compulsion (future).
3 An elliptical expression, with *nuestro* ('our') implied between the two words.

14 Cancellation of order

6 July 199-

Porzellanfabrik Hering
Langauer Allee 18
7000 Stuttgart
Germany

Dear Sirs

RE: ORDER NO. HGF/756

We recently placed an order for 60 bone china coffee sets (model 'Arcadia'). The order reference: HGF/756.

We regret that due to circumstances beyond our control, we now have to cancel the order. We apologize for any inconvenience this may cause you.

Yours faithfully

D. Grey

14 Anulando un pedido

Porcelanas Preciosas S.L.
Calle Rubina, 11
Murcia
España.   6.7.199-

Asunto: pedido No. HGF/756

Muy Sres nuestros:

En fecha reciente les hicimos un pedido de sesenta juegos de café de porcelana (modelo 'Arcadia') – no.[1] de referencia del pedido: HGF/756.

Lamentamos notificarles que debido a circunstancias ajenas a nuestra voluntad nos vemos obligados a anular dicho[2] pedido. Les rogamos sepan[3] disculparnos las molestias causadas.

Les saludamos cordialmente

                                                                D. Grey

1 Abbreviation of *número*.
2 *Dicho*: from *decir*: 'the said (order)'.
3 From *saber*: literally, 'We ask that you should know how to excuse us'.

15 Confirming a telephone order

18 January 199-

Henning & Söhne GmbH
Schillerstraße 45
4300 Essen
Germany

Dear Mr Hartmann

Following the visit of your representative Dieter Höne last week, we are pleased to confirm our telephone order for

    250 car seat covers, model AS/385/c

The total price of the order, including discount, is £4,600. Payment will follow immediately upon delivery. The covers should be delivered no later than Tuesday 3 February, to our warehouse on the Pennington Industrial Estate, Rochdale.

Yours sincerely

Derek Batty

15 Confirmando un pedido efectuado por teléfono

Henning & Söhne GmbH
Schillerstraße 45
4300 Essen
Alemania.   18.1.199-

Estimado Sr Hartmann:

Como continuación a la visita que nos hizo su representante Dieter Höne la semana pasada, nos es grato[1] confirmarle nuestro pedido telefónico de:

250 fundas de coche, modelo AS/385/c

El precio total del pedido, incluido descuento, asciende a 956.000 pesetas. El pago se efectuará inmediatamente después de la entrega del mismo.[2] Las fundas deberán entregarse para el martes día 3[3] de febrero en nuestro almacén ubicado[4] en el Polígono Industrial de Artiga, en Castellón.

Atentamente.[5]

Daniel Beltrán

1 Literally, 'it is pleasing for us'.
2 Referring to the order (*pedido*).
3 The word for day is invariably included before the date (e.g. *día* 3) in Spanish usage.
4 'Located'.
5 A minimal version of the final formal greeting.

16 Making an order for specific items of office equipment

7 July 199-

Your ref.
Our ref. HB/LP

Garzón e Hijos
Plaza de la Catedral 8
Bogotá

Dear Sir/Madam

Please supply the following items, using the Order Number E183, to the above address at your earliest convenience. Payment will be made within 14 days of receipt of your invoice and of the goods as ordered.

  6 artists' stools (aluminium)

20 sets of 5 painting brushes

10 reams of A5 drawing paper

  2 drawing tables: 2m × 1m

  1 Sanchix camera: FB4x model

  1 QRM computer: portable TGs model

Before you prepare and invoice us for these goods, please inform us by telex or phone of the cost per item, as in the past we have received unexpectedly high invoices.

We thank you in anticipation of your prompt reply.

Yours faithfully

Herberto Baza
Studio Supervisor

16 Solicitando un pedido de enseres de oficina

Garzón e hijos
Plaza de la Catedral, 8
Bogotá.   7.7.199-

Su ref.
Nuestra ref. HB/LP

Muy Sr mío/Sra mía:

        Agradeceremos que se sirvan anotar el siguiente pedido No. E183 que deberán enviar, lo antes posible, a la dirección arriba indicada. Deberá girar a nuestro cargo el importe de la remesa,[1] y el pago se efectuará catorce días después del recibo de la factura y de las mercancías.

  6 sillas de delineante (aluminio)

20 juegos de 5 pinceles

10 resmas de papel de dibujo A5

  2 mesas de delineante: 2m × 1m

  1 cámara fotográfica Sanchix: modelo FB4x

  1 ordenador QRM: modelo portátil TGs

Antes de preparar y girar a nuestro cargo el importe de la remesa, agradeceríamos nos informaran, por télex o por teléfono, del precio de cada artículo, ya que en el pasado hemos recibido facturas extremadamente[2] altas.

Confiando en su pronta entrega,[3] le doy las gracias anticipadas y le saludo[4] atentamente.

Herberto Baza
(Supervisor de Estudio)

1 Expanded from the English: 'the cost of the consignment should be charged to us'.
2 Literally, 'extremely'.
3 Implying reply about delivery.
4 Note first person verb form.

17 Acknowledgement of an order

17 September 199-

Mr Henry Putton
33 Flintway
West Ewell
Surrey
KT19 9ST

Dear Mr Putton

Thank you for your signed order given to our Advisor for a bed to be constructed to your specific requirements.

We shall now pass your order to our Design Department complete with the personal specification with which you have provided us.

Delivery time will be in approximately seven weeks and you will be advised of the exact date in due course.

Once again many thanks for your order.

Yours sincerely

Janet Craig
Customer Relations Manager

17 Acusando recibo de un pedido

Sr Henry Putton
33 Flintway
West Ewell
Surrey
KT19 9ST
Gran Bretaña.   17.9.199-

Estimado Sr Putton:

Le damos las gracias por el pedido que firmado entregó a nuestro asesor con el fin de que se le hiciera[1] una cama especial según sus requisitos.

Nos complace[2] comunicarle que dicho pedido se enviará a nuestro Departamento de Diseño junto con la especificación personal que usted nos ha proporcionado.

La entrega será aproximadamente dentro de siete semanas, aunque le notificaremos la fecha exacta a su debido tiempo.

Una vez más le agradecemos el pedido y nos despedimos[3] de usted muy atentamente.

Juanita Cabrera
Directora de Relaciones Públicas

1 Note use of reflexive *se* to express passive: 'bed to be constructed'.
2 A convention in correspondence: 'It pleases us to . . .'.
3 *Despedirse de*: 'to sign off', 'say goodbye'.

18 Payment of invoices

Letter accompanying payment

2 February 199-

Dr V Meyer
Neue Marktforschung GmbH
Kastanienallee 14
D–45023 Osnabrück
Germany

Dear Dr Meyer

I enclose an international money order to the value of 450DM as payment for the three market research reports on dairy products published by your organization this year.

As agreed during our telephone conversation on 15.1.199-, the sum enclosed includes postage.

I look forward to receiving the reports as soon as possible.

Yours sincerely

Maria Meller

Enc.

18 Pago de facturas

Carta acompañada de pago

Dr V. Meyer
Neue Marktforschung GmbH
Kastanienallee 14
D–45023 Osnabrück
Alemania.

2.2.199-

Estimado Dr Meyer:

Le adjunto[1] giro bancario internacional por valor de 450 marcos alemanes correspondiente al pago de los tres informes pertenecientes a la investigación del mercado de los productos lácteos publicados por su organización el presente año.

Según lo acordado[2] en nuestra conversación telefónica del 15.1.199-, en dicha cantidad va incluido el franqueo.[3]

Me veré muy complacida en recibir los informes cuanto antes.[4]

Sin otro particular, le saluda muy atentamente,

María Molina

Anexo

1 Note absence of article (*un/el*) in this typical usage of the verb *adjuntar* ('to enclose').
2 *Lo* plus past participle/adjective: a typical feature of the Spanish language – here 'that which is/has been agreed'.
3 *Franquear*: 'to pay postage'.
4 Alternatives: *cuanto antes, lo antes posible, lo más pronto posible.*

19 Payment of invoices

Request for deferral

4 March 199-

South East Finance Ltd
Alton Court
Cleeve Road
London
W11 1XR

Dear Sirs

RE: MAXITRUCK 2000

I refer to our recent agreement of 30 November 199- regarding payment for one 40-ton Maxitruck 2000.

As you will recall, we paid an initial instalment of £10,000 and agreed to 10 further monthly instalments of £3,000. The December and January instalments, as you will know, have been paid promptly.

However, owing to the serious economic situation we find ourselves in, we are at the moment unable to make payments as agreed. Because of our reduced cash flow we are unable to pay more than £2,000 a month. We would, therefore, appreciate the opportunity to discuss this matter with you and reach a mutually satisfactory arrangement.

Yours faithfully

Tom Page
Finance Manager

19 Pago de facturas

Petición de aplazamiento

South East Finance Ltd
Alton Court
Cleeve Road
London W11 1XR
Inglaterra.

4.3.199-

Asunto: Maxitruck 2000

Estimados señores:

Hago referencia a nuestro acuerdo del 30.11.199- sobre el pago de un Maxitruck 2000 de cuarenta toneladas.

Si ustedes recuerdan,[1] abonamos[2] un pago inicial de 10.000 libras esterlinas y acordamos abonar otros diez pagos mensuales de 3.000 libras cada uno. Los pagos correspondientes a diciembre y enero, como bien saben, los efectuamos sin demora.

Sin embargo, debido a la grave crisis económica en la que nos vemos sumergidos,[3] nos es de momento imposible[4] seguir efectuando los pagos según lo estipulado. Puesto que nuestro flujo de efectivo[5] está reducido, nos vemos en la imposibilidad de abonar más de 2.000 libras mensuales. Nos gustaría poder tratar de este tema con ustedes y poder llegar a un mutuo y satisfactorio arreglo.

Les saluda atentamente,

Tomás Patalote
Director de Finanzas

1 Literally, 'If you remember'.
2 *Abonamos, acordamos, efectuamos* are all past tense forms.
3 Literally, 'in which we see ourselves submerged' – a typically vivid expression in Spanish.
4 Inverted word order, as compared with English.
5 *Efectivo*: a standard reduced form (*dinero en efectivo*). Alternatives: (*el*) *cashflow* or (*el*) *flujo de caja*.

20 Payment of invoices

Refusal to pay

19 May 199-

Johnson (Builders) Ltd
Nugget Grove
Christchurch

Dear Sirs

RE: INVOICE NO. L28/4659

We refer to your invoice No. L28/4659 regarding repairs to the roof of workshop 17 at Heath End.

In spite of the repair work carried out by your employees the roof still leaked in a number of places during the recent rains, as a result causing a shut-down of the workshop for safety reasons.

We look forward to a speedy response in order to resolve this problem and assure you that your invoice will be paid as soon as this matter has been resolved to our satisfaction.

Yours faithfully

Daniela Fellowes
Deputy Director

20 Pago de facturas

Negándose a efectuar un pago

Hermanos Jordán
Calle de la Justicia, 23
Managua.   19.5.199-

Asunto: factura No. L28/4659

Muy Sres nuestros:

Hacemos referencia a su factura No. L28/4659 relacionada con las reparaciones del tejado del taller No. 17, ubicado en la zona franca este.

A pesar de las reparaciones efectuadas por sus empleados, el tejado ha seguido goteando por varios sitios durante las últimas lluvias, lo que[1] ha dado lugar al cierre definitivo del taller por razones de seguridad.

Les agradeceríamos una pronta respuesta para resolver este problema, y les aseguramos el pago de su factura tan pronto hayan resuelto[2] este asunto a nuestra satisfacción.

Reciban un cordial saludo[3]

Daniela Fonseca
Subdirectora

1 Referring to the fact of the roof leaking.
2 Subjunctive after *tan pronto*: indefinite future time.
3 A minimal final greeting.

21 Apologies for non-payment

17 August 199-

Mr I Sahani
Michigan Lake Trading Co.
974 South La Salle Street
Chicago
Illinois 60603
USA

Dear Mr Sahani

I refer to our telephone conversation yesterday.

I must once again apologize for the fact that you have not yet received payment for order no. 072230/5310.

Payment was duly authorized by me on the 10 July, but due to staff holidays the paperwork appears to have gone astray between our sales and finance departments.

We have now traced the relevant documentation and I can assure you that the matter is being attended to with the utmost urgency.

If you have not received payment by Monday, 22 August, I would be grateful if you would contact me immediately.

I apologize once again for the inconvenience this has caused you and assure you of our best intentions.

Yours sincerely

Timothy Morton

21 Pidiendo excusas por no efectuar un pago

Sr I. Sahani
Michigan Lake Trading Co.
974 South La Salle Street
Chicago
Illinois 60603
EE. UU.   17.8.199-

Estimado Sr Sahani:

Por la presente hago referencia a nuestra conversación telefónica de ayer.

Una vez más le pido sepa excusar el hecho de que usted no haya recibido todavía el pago relacionado con el pedido No. 072230/5310.

Dicho pago fue autorizado por mí el 10 de julio, pero debido a las vacaciones de nuestro personal la tramitación del mismo parece haberse extraviado entre el departamento de ventas y el de finanzas.

Ahora ya[1] hemos localizado la documentación pertinente, y le aseguro que estamos ocupándonos de este asunto con la mayor urgencia.

Si para[2] el lunes, 22 de agosto, no ha recibido el pago, le agradecería se pusiera en contacto conmigo inmediatamente.

Le ruego una vez más perdone[3] las molestias causadas, y le aseguramos nuestros mejores propósitos.

Reciba un atento saludo,

Tancredo Morales

1 *Ahora ya*: duplication of same idea for emphasis.
2 *Para* in time expressions implies 'by'/'before'.
3 The fourth example in the letter of subjunctive required in the subordinate clause.

22 Request for payment

15 May 199-

Huron Motor Factors
6732 John Street
Markham
Ontario
Canada L3R 1B4

Dear Sir

RE: INVOICE NO. JE/17193

As per our invoice JE/17193 of 13.3.199-, we supplied your Nashlee plant with 500 litres of AVC automotive base paint, payment due 60 days after receipt of our consignment.

This period of time has now elapsed and we request immediate settlement of the above invoice.

Yours faithfully

Duane Rogers
Accounts Manager

22 Petición de un pago

Servicio Carro Lindo
Avenida del Héroe, 65–68
Monterrey
México.   15.5.199-

Asunto: factura No. JE/17193

Muy Sr mío:

       Según nuestra factura JE/17193 del 13.3.199- suministramos a su fábrica de Monterrey 500 litros de pintura base AVC para autos – importe pagadero[1] sesenta días después del recibo del envío.

El estipulado período de tiempo ya ha transcurrido, y ahora nos vemos obligados a hacer requerimiento inmediato de dicho pago.

Sin otro particular, quedamos a la espera del mismo[2] y le saludamos atentamente.

Duane Rogers
(Responsable de pedidos)

1 *Importe pagadero*: 'amount payable'.
2 I.e. 'the said payment' (*dicho pago*).

23 Overdue account

First letter

31 May 199-

Lota (UK) Ltd
93 Armstrong Road
Dudley
West Midlands DY3 6EJ

Dear Sir

Arrears on Finance Agreement No. 261079

I am writing to advise you that your bankers have failed to remit the April instalment of £8,373 on the above agreement and as a result the account is now in arrears.

This has incurred an additional £460.50 in interest and administration charges.

Please advise your bank to transfer £8,833.50 to our account to bring your account up to date and enable us to remove it from our arrears listing.

Yours faithfully

Rosemary Wilson
Accounts Department

23 Pago atrasado

Primera notificación

Lota (España) S.A.
Carretera del Norte, 11
Burgos
España.   31.5.199-

Asunto: Atraso en el pago según acuerdo financiero No. 261079

Estimado señor:

          Le escribo para informarle que su banco no ha abonado la cuota,[1] que corresponde al mes de abril, de las 8.373 libras esterlinas según lo acordado, y por lo tanto dicho pago está ahora atrasado.

Esto ha originado gastos adicionales de intereses y de administración que ascienden a 460 libras con 50 peniques.

Le ruego informe a su banco que transfiera 8.833 libras con 50 peniques a nuestro favor con objeto de actualizar su cuenta y así poderle[2] eliminar de nuestra lista de atrasos.

Le saluda atentamente

Rosemary Wilson
(Depto.[3] de Contabilidad)

1 Instalment; also used for 'quota', 'share', 'fee', 'deposit', 'dues', 'premium'.
2 More correctly, *poder eliminarle*: 'be able to remove you'.
3 Abbreviation for *departamento*.

24 Overdue account

Final letter

12 June 199-

Lota (UK) Ltd
93 Armstrong Road
Dudley
West Midlands DY3 6EJ

Dear Sir

Arrears on Finance Agreement No. 261079

Our records show that despite our previous reminders, your account remains overdue.

We now insist that you clear the outstanding arrears by close of business on Friday, 26 June 199-.

If you should fail to comply with this request by the date specified, we would be obliged to rescind the contract and would take steps to recover our property.

Yours faithfully

Rosemary Wilson
Accounts Department

24 Pago atrasado

Última notificación

Lota (España) S.A.
Carretera del Norte, 11
Burgos
España.   12.6.199-

Asunto: Atraso en el pago según acuerdo financiero No. 261079

Estimado señor:

   Según apuntan nuestros registros contables, y a pesar de las notificaciones y advertencias[1] enviadas, su pago sigue pendiente.

Ha llegado el momento de insistirle que usted debe liquidar[2] dicho pago para el viernes 26 de junio de 199- para la hora de cierre.

Si no cumpliera con esta petición para la fecha y hora estipulada, nos veríamos obligados a la rescisión del contrato, y tomaríamos medidas para recuperar los pagos pendientes.[3]

Le saluda atentamente.

Rosemary Wilson
(Departamento de Contabilidad)

1 *Advertencias*: 'warnings'.
2 'To settle, to pay off'. Alternatives: *pagar, abonar, saldar.*
3 'Outstanding payments'.

25 Job advertisement

Letter to newspaper

14 December 199-

H J Marketing Services
County House
53 Stukely Street
Twickenham TW1 7LA

Dear Sir

Please would you insert the attached job advertisement in the January issues of *East European Marketing Monthly* and *Food Industry Digest*.

As usual, we would like a quarter-page ad, set according to our house style.

Please invoice payment in the usual way.

Yours faithfully

Philip Redmond
Personnel Manager

Enc.

25 Anuncio de puesto de trabajo

Carta a revista

H.J. Marketing Services
County House
53 Stukely Street
Twickenham TW1 7LA
Inglaterra.   14.12.199-

Muy señor nuestro:

Le ruego inserte[1] en los números de enero de las revistas *East European Marketing Monthly* y *Food Industry Digest* el adjunto anuncio de puesto de trabajo.

Como de costumbre, deseamos que dicho anuncio ocupe un cuarto de página y figure según el estilo de esta empresa que le adjuntamos.[2]

Sírvase enviar factura según acostumbra.[3]

Sin otro particular, le saluda

                                        Felipe Remedios
                                        (Jefe de Personal)

Anexo

1 This, together with three further examples in this brief letter, well illustrates the frequency and importance of subjunctive forms in Spanish-language correspondence: where one party is requesting the other to act, the desired outcomes are expressed as hypotheses.
2 Literally, 'the style of this company which we enclose to you'.
3 Again, note the elliptical style of much correspondence, omitting words obvious to writer and addressee.

26 Job advertisement

We are now expanding our operations in Eastern Europe and require experienced people within the food processing industry who are looking for an opportunity to sell products of leading Hungarian and Bulgarian food companies. The products are of good quality and already enjoy a substantial international reputation.

Salary for the above position is negotiable dependent upon experience and qualifications. A competitive benefits package is offered.

For further details and application form please write to the Personnel Manager, EEF Ltd, 34–40 Roman Road, Epsom, Surrey, KT72 7EF, quoting reference HB/127.

Closing date: 14 February 199-.

26 Anuncio de puesto de trabajo

Con motivo[1] de la expansión de nuestras operaciones en la Europa del Este, necesitamos personal experto en el área de la industria de transformación de alimentos, e interesado en la oportunidad de vender productos procedentes[2] de importantes empresas alimenticias de Hungría y Bulgaria. Los productos, que son de buena calidad, gozan ya de sustancial reputación internacional.[3]

Salario a negociar según experiencia y cualificaciones. Se ofrece un competitivo conjunto de beneficios.

Para obtener mayor información y hoja de solicitud de empleo, sírvase escribir al Encargado de Personal, EEFSA, Calle Mayor 34–40, Sevilla, España; referencia HB/127.

Fecha de cierre: 14 de febrero de 199-

1 Expressing purpose rather than time.
2 I.e. exports from Hungary and Bulgaria.
3 Alternatively, and perhaps more likely: *tienen mucha fama*.

27 Asking for further details and application form

14 January 199-

EEF Ltd
34–40 Roman Road
Epsom
Surrey KT72 7EF

Dear Sir

REF. HB/127

I would be grateful if you could send me further details and an application form for the post of sales manager advertised in this month's issue of the journal *East European Marketing Monthly.*

Yours faithfully

Lauren Russell (Ms)

27 Pidiendo información e impreso de solicitud para un puesto de trabajo

Encargado de Personal

EEFSA
Calle Mayor, 34–40
Sevilla
España.   el 14 de enero de 199-

Ref. HB/127

Muy señor mío:

Le agradecería me enviara más información, así como impreso de solicitud, para el puesto de director de ventas aparecido en el número de este mes de la revista *East European Marketing Monthly*.

Le saluda cordialmente.

Lauren Russell (Srta)

28 Job application

25 January 199-

Black's (Automotive) Ltd
18 Dawson Street
Birmingham
B24 4SU

Dear Sir

I am applying for the post of market research officer advertised in the *Guardian* on 21 January 199-.

I graduated from Chiltern University in June with an upper second class degree in European Business. The following January I was awarded the Diploma of the Chartered Institute of Marketing. On my degree course I specialized in market research and did a one-year work placement with Cox, Paton and Taylor in London.

Since leaving university I have been employed as a market research assistant in the Quantocks Tourist Agency. I am now seeking an opportunity to apply the knowledge and skills I have acquired in a larger, more market-orientated organization.

I enclose a CV and the names of two referees. I would be grateful if you would not contact my current employer without prior reference to me.

Yours faithfully

Michael Westwood

Encs

28 Solicitud de empleo

El Director de Personal
Automotriz S.A.
Cruce Ducal, 1
Teruel
España.   el 25 de enero de 199-

Estimado señor:

Me complace solicitar el puesto de investigador de mercado,
anunciado en *El País*[1] del 21.1.199-.

El pasado junio terminé mis estudios de licenciatura en la Universidad de
Chiltern, donde cursé la carrera[2] de Ciencias Empresariales Europeas,
obteniendo matrícula de honor. En enero del año siguiente[3] me otorgaron el
Diploma del Instituto de Márketing.[4] Durante los estudios de licenciatura me
especialicé en la Investigación de Mercado y trabajé, durante un año y como
parte integral de mis estudios, para la empresa Cox, Paton y Taylor de Londres.

Desde que terminé mis estudios universitarios estoy trabajando como ayudante
de investigador de mercado para la Agencia de Turismo Quantocks. Ahora
quisiera[5] poner en práctica, sirviendo a una organización más grande y más
orientada hacia el mercado, los conocimientos y las destrezas que he ido
adquiriendo.

Adjunto C.V. y los nombres de dos personas que pueden proporcionarle
referencias mías. Le agradecería no se pusiera en contacto con mi jefe actual sin
antes contar conmigo.[6]

Le saluda cordialmente.

                                                        Michael Westwood

Anexos

1 Spain's major national daily paper.
2 Literally, 'where I followed the course...'.
3 I.e. **this** year.
4 In Latin America the term *mercadeo* is more frequent.
5 'I would like'.
6 Literally, 'without before counting with me'.

29 Curriculum vitae

Surname:	Cording
First names:	Donald Maurice
Date of Birth:	18 March 1959

QUALIFICATIONS: BA (Hons) Business Studies (Leeds, 1981)
MBA (Warwick, 1985)

CURRENT EMPLOYMENT:
(Sept. 1988 to the present) Marketing Manager, Cockpit Industries Ltd,
8 Wendover Road, Accrington, Lancs. BB7 2RH

PREVIOUS EMPLOYMENT:

(a) Jan. 1986–Sept. 1988: Marketing Assistant,
Spurlands Ltd, 71 Misbourne Road,
Northallerton, Yorks. DL5 7YL

(b) Oct. 1981–Dec. 1985: Marketing Assistant,
Tutton Enterprises Ltd, Wye House,
Cores End, Wolverhampton WV6 8AE

(c) Sept. 1979–July 1980: Sales Assistant,
J V Ansell & Co., Greenaway Avenue,
Leek, Staffs. ST15 4EH

29 Curriculum vitae

Apellido:[1]   Cording
Nombres: Donald Maurice
Fecha de nacimiento: 18.03.1959

ESTUDIOS: Licenciatura en Ciencias Empresariales,
                                    Leeds,[2] 1981

                                    MBA, Warwick, 1985

PUESTO ACTUAL:
Setiembre[3] 1988 –   Director de Márketing, Cockpit Industries
                                    Ltd, 8 Wendover Road, Accrington, Lancs.
                                    BB7 2RH, Inglaterra.

PUESTOS ANTERIORES:
a) Enero 1986 – Setiembre 1988:   Ayudante de Márketing,
                                    Spurlands Ltd, 71 Misbourne Road,
                                    Northallerton, Yorks. DL5 7YL,
                                    Inglaterra.

b) Octubre 1981 – Diciembre 1985: Ayudante de Márketing,
                                    Tutton Enterprises Ltd, Wye House,
                                    Cores End, Wolverhampton WV6 8AE,
                                    Inglaterra.

c) Setiembre 1979 – Julio 1980:   Ayudante de ventas,
                                    J.V. Ansell & Co., Greenaway Avenue,
                                    Leek, Staffs. ST15 4EH,
                                    Inglaterra.

1 Spanish people, of course, have two surnames: one each from mother and father.
2 Evidently, from the University (see below, also, Warwick).
3 Also spelt *septiembre*; months in Spanish are still usually spelt in normal text with lower
   case initial letter.

30 Unsolicited letter of application

5 November 199-

Executive Agency plc
22 Ellison Place
London WC1B 1DP

Dear Sirs

I have recently returned to Britain after working in Canada and the Gulf States for the last 15 years.

I spent five years working in Canada as chief financial accountant of Bourges-Canada in Montreal, before moving to the Gulf. I have worked as financial director for Jenkins-Speller for the last ten years. During this period the company's number of clients as well as its turnover have quadrupled.

I have returned to Britain for family reasons and I am now seeking an appropriate position in a company that can capitalize on my expertise in financial management and strategy.

I enclose a detailed CV for your further information and look forward to hearing from you soon.

Yours faithfully

Roger Bennett

Enc.

30 Solicitando empleo no anunciado

Agencia Mérito[1]
Plaza de los Héroes, 7
Santiago de Chile. 5.11.199-

Estimados señores:

Hace poco tiempo que he regresado a Chile después de haber trabajado en el Canadá[2] y en los países del Golfo Pérsico durante quince años.

Durante cinco años trabajé en el Canadá de jefe de contabilidad para la empresa Bourges-Canadá, en Montreal, antes de trasladarme al Golfo. Durante los diez últimos años he trabajado en el puesto de director financiero para Jenkins-Speller, período en el que tanto el número de clientes como el volumen de facturación de dicha empresa se ha visto[3] cuadruplicado.

He regresado a Chile por razones familiares, y ahora busco un puesto de trabajo apropiado en una empresa, la cual pueda sacar partido de la experiencia en dirección y estrategia financiera[4] que poseo.

Para mayor información adjunto C.V.[5] detallado, y espero tener pronto noticias suyas.

Atentamente suyo,[6]

Rodrigo Benet

Anexo

1 A private employment agency.
2 Canada is one of several country names invariably accompanied in Spanish by the definite article.
3 A singular verb is frequently used where a plural might more correctly reflect two (or more) subjects.
4 Again, plural (*financieras*) would be more accurate if it refers to both *dirección* and *estrategia*.
5 In Colombia, for example, the CV is called *hoja de vida*.
6 'Yours' ('faithfully', 'sincerely').

31 Interview invitation

12 February 199-

Ms F Jones
23 Park View
Colchester
Essex CO4 3RN

Dear Ms Jones

Ref. PS/2021: Personnel assistant

Interviews for the above position will take place on Friday, 22 February 199-, beginning at 10 a.m.

We expect to conclude the interviews after lunch, at approximately 2.30 p.m.

Please confirm whether you will attend the interview.

Yours sincerely

Mr C Smith
Personnel Officer

31 Llamada a una entrevista

Srta F. Jarpa
Edificio Violeta Ramos
Planta 1, D, izq.[1]
Glorieta del Sol
Mendoza.

12 de febrero de 199-

Ref. PS/2021

Asunto: Ayudante de personal

Estimada Srta Jarpa:

Las entrevistas para el puesto arriba indicado tendrán lugar el viernes, 22 de febrero de 199-, dando comienzo a las 10 de la mañana.

Esperamos terminar dichas entrevistas después del almuerzo, aproximadamente a las 14.30h.[2]

Sírvase informarnos si asistirá a la misma.[3]

Le saluda atentamente,

Sra C. Salas
Jefa[4] de Personal

1 '1st floor, flat D, on the left'.
2 Also expressed as *las dos y media de la tarde*.
3 *Misma*: referring to the interview (plural in antecedent). *Confirmarnos si/que*: an alternative to '*informarnos . . .*'.
4 A now commonly accepted feminine form of the masculine *jefe*.

32 Favourable reply to job application

26 March 199-

Mrs L Flint
7 Fisherman's Way
Okehampton
Devon EX12 0YX

Dear Mrs Flint

I am writing to offer you formally the position of personal assistant to the operations director at Farnbury.

As discussed at the interview the normal working hours are 8.30 a.m.–5 p.m., Monday to Friday, although the position requires a flexible approach and on occasions you will be expected to work outside these times. The annual salary is £18,000.

You will receive further details should you accept the position.

Please confirm in writing by first post, Monday 3 April at the latest, whether you accept the offer of the position.

Yours sincerely

Oliver Ross
Personnel Manager

32 Respuesta favorable a una solicitud de empleo

Sra L. Flint
7 Fisherman's Way
Okehampton
Devon EX12 0YX
Reino Unido.   26.3.199-

Estimada Sra Flint:

Le escribo para ofrecerle oficialmente el puesto de ayudante de personal de nuestro director de operaciones en Inglaterra.

Según lo acordado en la entrevista, el horario laboral es de 8.30 de la mañana a 5[1] de la tarde, de lunes a viernes; no obstante,[2] el puesto requiere flexibilidad de horario y habrá ocasiones en las que tenga[3] que trabajar horas distintas a las estipuladas. Percibirá[4] un salario de 18.000 libras esterlinas anuales.

En caso de que acepte dicho puesto, le remitiremos información más detallada.

Le ruego nos confirme por escrito, a más tardar[5] para el primer reparto del lunes 3 de abril, si acepta la oferta que le proponemos.

Sin otro particular, le saluda muy atentamente,

Orlando Ríos
(Encargado de Personal)

1 Note omission of article *las* in the times of day.
2 Literally, 'notwithstanding'.
3 The subjunctive is used because the situation alluded to is hypothetical.
4 A frequent alternative to *ganar* and *cobrar* ('to earn').
5 Literally, 'at most to delay'.

33 Unfavourable reply to job application

11 July 199-

Mr R Smith
15 Adams Way
Reading
Berks
RG23 6WD

Dear Mr Smith

RE: POSITION AS SALES DIRECTOR

I am writing to inform you that your application was unsuccessful on this occasion.

Thank you for the interest you have shown in our company and we wish you every success with your career.

Yours sincerely

Raymond Dawson
Personnel Manager

33 Respuesta desfavorable a una solicitud de empleo

Sr R. Smith
15 Adams Way
Reading
Berks
RG23 6WD
Inglaterra.

11.7.199-

Asunto: puesto de director de ventas

Estimado Sr Smith:

Lamento[1] informarle que, en esta ocasión, su solicitud de empleo ha sido rechazada.[2]

Le agradezco el interés que usted ha mostrado por nuestra empresa y le deseo mucho éxito en su carrera.

Atentamente le saluda,

Ramón Díaz
(Encargado de Personal)

1 'I regret': paraphrased in the Spanish version.
2 The word 'rejected' is a paraphrase in the Spanish version.

34 Requesting a reference for a job applicant

Your ref. AS/
Our ref. FG/JL

1 May 199-

The Manager
First Class Bank
1–6, King's Square
BURY

Dear Mr Swift

RE: MISS STEPHANIE BOSSOM

This branch of the Safety First has recently received an application for employment as an accounts clerk from Ms Stephanie Bossom. She has quoted your name as a referee to whom we might address ourselves in the event of our wishing to interview her.

I believe that Ms Bossom has been working in your bank for several years and that her desire to change employment is prompted largely by her intention to marry and settle in this area. From her application she appears to be the ideal candidate for this company; therefore we should be most grateful if you could confirm the impression we have of her in writing (or by fax if possible) as soon as is convenient.

Please feel free to comment on any aspect of Ms Bossom's work that you deem to be of likely interest to us.

I thank you in advance for your cooperation.

Yours sincerely

Frank Graham
Branch Manager

34 Pidiendo referencias sobre una persona que solicita un puesto de trabajo

The Manager
First Class Bank
1–6, Kings Square
Bury

Su ref: AS/
Nra ref: FG/JL

1.5.199-

Estimado Sr Swift:

Esta sucursal[1] de la Safety First ha recibido recientemente de la señorita Stephanie Bossom una solicitud para un puesto de trabajo como empleada del[2] departamento de contabilidad. Dicha[3] señorita nos ha proporcionado su nombre de usted como referencia y persona[4] a quien pudiéramos[5] dirigirnos en caso de[6] querer hacerle una entrevista.

Me consta que la señorita Bossom lleva trabajando[7] varios años en su banco y que su deseo de cambiar de puesto de trabajo ha surgido principalmente en vistas a[8] su próximo matrimonio y su intención de fijar su residencia en esta zona. Según se desprende[9] de su solicitud, parece ser la candidata idónea para esta empresa; por lo tanto le agradeceríamos a usted nos confirmara[10] por escrito (o bien por fax) a la mayor brevedad posible la impresión que tenemos de ella.

No dude en hacer cualquier observación pertinente al trabajo de la señorita Bossom que le parezca nos pudiera[11] interesar.

Agradeciéndole de antemano su cooperación, le saluda atentamente

Frank Graham
(Director de sucursal)

1 The standard term for a branch of a business.
2 Alternatively, *en el* ...
3 *Dicha*: 'the above mentioned'.
4 *Referencia* alone does not necessarily imply the human nature of 'referee'; hence the inclusion of *persona*.
5 Imperfect subjunctive, expressing possibility.
6 Here, followed by the infinitive because all verbs in this clause have the same subject ('us': i.e. Safety First).
7 *Llevar* + gerund: to express continuity from past to present.
8 'With a view to', 'in view of'.
9 *Desprenderse*: 'to conclude, to infer'.
10 Imperfect subjunctive after main verb conditional tense.
11 Note: the third of three subjunctive forms in one sentence.

35 Providing a positive reference for an employee

2 April 199-

Your ref. FG/JL
Our ref. AS/MN

Mr F Graham
Safety First Assurance plc
12, Bright Street
Lancaster

Dear Mr Graham

MS STEPHANIE BOSSOM

I hasten to reply to your letter requesting a reference for Ms Stephanie Bossom. Please accept my apologies for not being able to fax my reply, but at present we are experiencing problems with the machine.

Yes, Stephanie has been an ideal employee who started with us as an office junior straight from school and has been promoted on several occasions in recognition of her work. I understand her reasons for wishing to leave and I would have promoted her again very soon, were she to have stayed with us.

You will see from her application that she has sat and passed a number of professional examinations over the last two years. During that time she has taken responsibility for supervising the progress of trainees and has been involved in new initiatives relating to our office systems.

You will find Stephanie a pleasant, willing and talented person. You can rely upon her to carry out her professional duties to the best of her ability at all times.

I hope you will be able to offer her the post, which you imply is likely in your initial letter.

Yours sincerely

Alan Swift
(Manager, Town Centre Branch)

35 Respuesta favorable a una petición de referencias

Sr F. González
Jefe de Personal
Delta S.A.
Calle del Carmen, 36
Logroño
España.

2.4.199-

Su ref. FG/JL
Nuestra ref. AS/MN

Estimado Sr González:

Me apresuro a dar contestación a su carta en la que me pedía le proporcionara referencias de la señorita Stephanie Bossom. Le ruego sepa disculpar no le haya podido enviar la contestación por fax, debido a los problemas que nos han surgido con el aparato.

Ciertamente, le confirmo que Stephanie Bossom ha sido una empleada modelo,[1] la cual empezó a trabajar con nosotros en capacidad de oficinista subalterna recién terminada su escolarización, y en reconocimiento a su trabajo ha sido ascendida de puesto varias veces. Soy consciente de las razones que la mueven a cambiarse de puesto,[2] y de haberse quedado con nosotros la hubiera vuelto a ascender muy pronto.

Por su solicitud observará que, durante los últimos dos años, la Srta Bossom ha superado una serie de exámenes y pruebas profesionales. Durante ese período de tiempo se ha responsabilizado de supervisar el progreso de las aprendices, y ha llevado a cabo nuevas iniciativas relacionadas con el sistema de esta oficina.

Usted comprobará que Stephanie es agradable, aplicada y talentosa; en ella se puede confiar el llevar a cabo sus tareas profesionales en todo momento.

Espero que usted pueda ofrecerle el puesto, según afirma de esta posibilidad en su primera carta.

Atentamente le saluda,

Alan Swift
(Director)

1 *Modelo* is a noun acting as an adjective, so it does not change to agree grammatically with *empleada*.
2 ('To leave') literally, 'to change job'.

36 Acceptance letter

20 July 199-

Melton's Motor Factors Ltd
63 Station Road
Thirsk
N. Yorkshire
YO9 4YN

Dear Sir

Thank you for your letter of 17 July offering me the post of parts manager.

I am delighted to tell you that I accept your offer.

Yours sincerely

Andrew Camp

36 Aceptando un puesto de trabajo

Sr S. Palacios
Coches Real S.A.
Avenida Manresa
Estepona.   el veinte de julio, 199-

Muy señor mío:

Le agradezco su atta.[1] carta del 17 de julio en la que me ofrece el puesto de gerente del departamento de piezas.

Me es grato comunicarle que acepto dicho cargo.[2]

Le saluda atentamente,

                                                      Andrés del Campo

1   Abbreviation of *atenta*.
2   *Cargo*: 'job, position'.

37   Contract of employment

Dear

Following recent discussions we are pleased to offer you employment at our Company as Area Manager on the following terms and conditions:-

Remuneration
Your salary will be £15,000 per annum plus commission on the basis we have already discussed with you. As with all our staff, your salary will be paid monthly on the last Thursday in each month, your first review being in July 199-.

Notice
As with all our staff, you will be employed for an initial trial period of six months, during which time either you or we may terminate your appointment at any time upon giving seven days' notice in writing to the other. If we are satisfied with your performance during the trial period, once it is completed we will immediately confirm your appointment as a permanent member of our staff and the seven days' period of notice referred to above, will be increased to one month.

Sickness Pay
During any reasonable absence for illness the Company, at its discretion, will make up the amount of your National Insurance Benefit to the equivalent of your normal salary, although this will be essentially relative to your length of service.

Holidays
Your normal paid holiday entitlement will be 20 working days in a full year, the holiday year running from 1 January to 31 December.

Car
We will provide you with a suitable Company car (cost circa £14,000), which is to be mainly for your business use but also for your private use. The Company will meet all normal running expenses associated with the car such as road tax, insurance, repairs, servicing and petrol.

Pensions
The Company operates a Pension Plan. You can either decide to join the Company Scheme after six months' service at the Scheme's next anniversary date (6 July 199-), or alternatively choose a Personal Pension Plan to which the Company would contribute.

Hours
Normal office hours are from 9.00 a.m. to 5.15 p.m. from Monday to Friday, with one hour for lunch. However, it is probable that additional calls will be made upon your time.

Grievance and Disciplinary Procedure
Should you wish to seek redress for any grievance relating to your employment, you should refer, as appropriate, either to the Company Secretary or to the Managing Director. Matters involving discipline will be dealt with in as fair and equitable a manner as possible.

37 Contrato de trabajo

Estimado/a

Según lo tratado[1] recientemente, nos complace ofrecerle el puesto de Director/a de Zona en nuestra empresa bajo las siguientes condiciones.[2]

Remuneración
De acuerdo con lo acordado recientemente, usted percibirá un salario de 3.120.000 pesetas anuales más comisión. El salario se le abonará, como al resto de nuestro personal, el último jueves de mes, efectuándose la primera revisión del mismo[3] en julio de 199-.

Despido/Dimisión[4]
El período inicial de prueba de empleo que se lleva a cabo con todo nuestro personal es de seis meses; durante este plazo bien usted o nosotros podemos terminar el contrato en cualquier momento, mediante previa notificación hecha por escrito siete días antes del mismo.[5] Si estamos satisfechos con el cumplimiento de su cargo durante el período de prueba, una vez cumplido éste,[6] le comunicaremos inmediatamente la inclusión permanente a nuestra plantilla,[7] y el período de notificación de cese, al que nos referíamos anteriormente, quedará prolongado a un mes.

Subsidio de enfermedad
Durante un período razonable debido a enfermedad la Empresa completará, a su discreción, la cantidad de prestaciones a la Seguridad Social equivalentes a su salario normal, aunque esto será esencialmente relativo a la antigüedad.[8]

Vacaciones
Usted tendrá derecho a veinte días laborables al año de vacaciones pagadas, estando éstas comprendidas entre el 1 de enero y el 31 de diciembre.

Vehículo
La empresa le proporcionará un automóvil adecuado (cuyo coste está estimado en aproximadamente 2.900.000 ptas), que podrá utilizar para su trabajo y uso particular. Nosotros nos haremos cargo de cualquier gasto relacionado con dicho vehículo, tal como impuesto de circulación, seguro, reparaciones, mantenimiento y gasolina.

Pensión
La Empresa dispone de un Plan de Pensiones. Usted puede acogerse al Plan de la Empresa después de seis meses de servicio a partir del próximo aniversario del plan, es decir el próximo 6 de julio, o por otra parte, puede escoger un Plan Personal de Pensión al que la Empresa contribuiría.

Horario
El horario laboral de oficina es de 9 de la mañana a 5.15 de la tarde, de lunes a viernes, disponiendo de una hora para el almuerzo. No obstante, es probable que tenga que trabajar horas extra.[9]

Health & Safety at Work Act

A copy of the Staff Notice issued under the Health & Safety at Work etc. Act 1974 will be given to you on the first day of your employment. Your acceptance of the appointment will be deemed to constitute your willingness to comply with these regulations.

Start Date

The date on which your employment is to commence remains to be agreed by the Company. We look forward to establishing a mutually acceptable date as soon as possible.

Would you kindly provide us with your acceptance of this offer of employment by signing and returning to us the enclosed duplicate copy of this letter.

We trust that you will have a long, happy and successful association with our Company.

Yours sincerely

B. Foster
Managing Director

Enc.

4.6.199-

Juicio de faltas y disciplina

En caso de querer desagraviar cualquier queja relacionada con su trabajo, deberá dirigirse, oportunamente, bien al Secretario de la Empresa o al Director-Gerente. Los asuntos relacionados con la disciplina se tratarán de la manera más justa y equitativa posible.

Higiene y Seguridad

El primer día de trabajo con nosotros, le será entregada una copia del libro que distribuimos a nuestro personal sobre la Ley de Higiene y Seguridad en el Trabajo (1974). El aceptar el puesto de trabajo ofrecido conlleva[10] el deseo del cumplimiento de dicho reglamento.

Fecha de comienzo de empleo

La fecha en la que ha de comenzar a trabajar con nosotros está por determinar por la Empresa, pero esperamos que usted y la Empresa acordarán dicha fecha[11] lo antes posible.

Le rogamos nos proporcione aceptación de esta oferta de trabajo firmando y remitiéndonos[12] la copia de esta carta que se adjunta.

Esperamos que su relación con esta Empresa sea larga, feliz y provechosa.

Le saluda atentamente,

B. Fernández
Director Gerente

(4.6.199-)

Anexo

1 Impersonal expression: 'that which was dealt with'.
2 In Spanish the word for 'terms' is synonymous with 'conditions' (*condiciones*); though *términos* might also be used.
3 *Mismo*: referring to *salario*.
4 *Despido*: dismissal. *Dimisión*: resignation. See *cese* (below): more generally, notice of both kinds.
5 *Mismo*: referring here to act of terminating the contract.
6 Literally, 'once accomplished this'.
7 This word can mean 'staff', 'workforce' or 'team'.
8 *Antigüedad*: in this specific context: 'years of service'; elsewhere: 'age' or 'antiquity'.
9 'Overtime'; also *horas extras*.
10 Literally, 'brings with it'.
11 'The said (i.e. agreed between both parties) date'.
12 The present participle/gerund (*firmando y remitiéndonos*) includes the amplified meaning of 'by .. -ing'.

38 Enquiring about regulations for purchase of property abroad (memo)

<u>Internal memorandum</u>

From: Terry Baddison (Customer Services)
To: Guillermo Estuardos (Legal Department)

Date: 9 September 199-

Message: I urgently need some information on current rules and regulations concerning the purchase and renting of property in Spain. We have some clients interested in the new complex at Carboneras, but there seems to be doubt over whether they can sublet part of the premises without paying local tax on the rental. Can you check this out ASAP?

P.S. I'm in the office every afternoon this week.

Terry

38 Pidiendo información sobre adquisición inmobiliaria en el extranjero (comunicado interno)

Comunicado interno

De: Terry Baddison (Servicios para el cliente)

A: Guillermo Estuardos (Asesoría[1] Jurídica)

9 de setiembre de 199-

Necesito urgentemente información sobre reglamento[2] vigente acerca de la compra y alquiler de inmuebles en España. Algunos de nuestros clientes están interesados en la nueva urbanización[3] en Carboneras, pero parece que hay dudas sobre si pueden subarrendar una parte de la propiedad sin pagar impuestos municipales en el alquiler. ¿Puedes comprobarlo cuanto antes?

P.D.[4] Esta semana estoy en la oficina todas las tardes.

                                                                                    Terry

1 More specifically: 'Consultancy'.
2 The omission of the article (*el*) prior to the key word (*reglamento*) would be normal in a brief communication.
3 The *urbanización*, a new housing estate for tourist or permanent accommodation, has been a typical feature of post-1950s economic development in Spain; alternatively, *complejo* for a smaller, more recent or more tourist-based location.
4 *Post data*: 'P.S.'

39 Advising of delay in delivery (telex)

TELEX:	Expofrut (Almería, Spain) to Henshaw Bros. (Wolverhampton, England)
Subject:	Delay in delivery
Sender:	Pablo López
Addressee:	Mary Henshaw
Date:	14 December 199-
Message:	APOLOGIES FOR FAILING TO DELIVER USUAL ORDER THIS WEEK.

DOCKS STRIKE CALLED FROM TODAY THROUGHOUT SPAIN.

YOUR CONSIGNMENT OF FRUIT AND VEGETABLES ON QUAYSIDE. STILL POSSIBLE TO SEND GOODS BY ROAD, BUT COULD NOT GUARANTEE DELIVERY BY WEEKEND.

INFORM BY TELEPHONE (00 3451 947583) THIS P.M. IF TO PROCEED WITH ORDER BY ROAD.

REGARDS

Pablo López
(Export Manager)

39 Notificando el retraso de una entrega (télex)

TELEX

Para: Henshaw Bros (Wolverhampton, Inglaterra)

De :   Expofrut (Almería, España)

Asunto: Retraso de entrega

Remitente: Pablo López

Destinataria: Mary Henshaw

14 de diciembre, 199-

Mensaje[1]

Disculpen no entregar, como de costumbre, pedido esta semana. Retraso debido

a huelga portuaria convocada hoy por toda España.

Su consignación de frutas y verduras en el muelle. Posibilidad de enviar

mercancías por carretera, pero no garantizar entrega para fin de semana.

Notifiquen por teléfono (00 3451 947583) esta tarde si quiere pedido por

carretera.

Saludos.

Firma,[2]

Pablo López
(Director de Exportación)

1 As a telex, the message is expressed in elliptical terms: omitting articles and some verbs, in particular. The main verbs relating to the sender's actions are expressed in the infinitive (*entregar, enviar, garantizar*); those relating to the addressee's, in the command/imperative form (*Disculpen, Notifiquen*).
2 Literally, 'he signs'.

40 Seeking clarification of financial position (fax)

To: Accounts Section, MULTIBANK,
        Prince's Square, Crewe

From: John Turket, PERLOANS
        High Street, Tamworth

Date: 4 November 199-
No. of pages, including this: 1

Dear Sir

This company has been approached today by a Mr Alan Thomas, who wishes to secure a loan in order to finance a family visit to relatives living overseas. Mr Thomas has given his approval to my contacting your branch of Multibank, where he holds two accounts, in order to verify and clarify information he has already proffered about his financial position.

Once you have satisfied yourselves that Mr Thomas is willing that you divulge facts about his finances, could you please provide the following information?

1 Has Mr Thomas incurred major overdrafts since 1990?

2 Do both Mr Thomas and his wife have salary cheques paid directly each month into their current account?

3 Does your bank believe that Mr Thomas will be able to repay a £3,000 loan to Perloans over 3 years from July 199-?

We hope you are in a position to respond to our request, and thank you for your assistance in this matter.

Yours faithfully

John Turket
Loans Manager

40 Solicitando aclaración sobre situación financiera (fax)

FAX

A: Multibank, Sección de Contaduría,
        Plaza del Príncipe,
        Madrid, España.

De: John Turket, Perloans,
        High Street, Tamworth, Inglaterra.

Fecha: 4 de noviembre, 199-
No. de páginas, incluida ésta: 1

Muy Sr mío:

El Sr Alan Thomas se ha puesto en contacto con esta compañía hoy con objeto de conseguir un préstamo[1] para financiar una visita a familiares que viven en la América Latina. El Sr Thomas está de acuerdo con que yo me ponga en contacto con su sucursal de Multibank, en la cual tiene abiertas dos cuentas, y así verificar y aclarar la información ya ofrecida por él acerca de su situación financiera.

Una vez convencidos ustedes[2] de que el Sr Thomas está dispuesto a que ustedes revelen su situación financiera, ¿podrían facilitar la siguiente información a esta casa?[3]

1   ¿Ha contraído el Sr Thomas algún saldo deudor importante desde 199-?
2   ¿A los Sres Thomas les domicilian[4] mensualmente sus salarios respectivos en su cuenta corriente?
3   ¿Piensa su banco que el Sr Thomas puede llegar a pagar a Perloans un préstamo de 3.000 libras esterlinas, por un período de tres años, a partir de julio de 199-?

Esperamos que usted se encuentre en posición de dar contestación a nuestra petición, y le agradecemos su colaboración en este asunto.

Le saluda atentamente,

John Turket
(Gerente de Préstamos)

1   Alternatives: *crédito, empréstito.*
2   Note change to plural (*ustedes*) and subsequent reversion to singular (*usted*).
3   *Casa*: 'company', 'business', 'branch'.
4   *Domiciliar*: 'to pay direct into an account', 'to lodge'. The subject of the verb here is unstated third person plural 'they', implying the Thomas's employers.

41 Reporting to client on availability of particular property (fax)

To: Lilian Topcopy
        Trendset Printers
From: Dorothy Russell
        Smith & Jones

Date: 6 September 199-

No. of pages, including this: 1

Re: Office for lease

Dear Lilian

I am faxing you urgently to let you know that office premises have just become available in the area of town you told me that you liked. The lease on a street-front shop with upstairs office has been cancelled early by another client, who is moving south. If you would like to see the property, please get back to us this afternoon and we will arrange a visit.

Best wishes

Dorothy Russell

41 Informando a un cliente sobre disponibilidad de una determinada propiedad (fax)

FAX

A: Liliana Copias
       Imprenta Progre

De: Dorothy Russell
       Smith & Jones

6/9/9-

N°. de páginas, incluida ésta: 1

Asunto: Arriendo de oficina

Estimada Liliana:

Te envío este fax urgente para que sepas[1] que acaban de quedar libres locales[2] de oficinas en la zona que me dijiste te gustaba. El alquiler de una tienda que da a la calle,[3] y con oficina en la parte de arriba, ha sido cancelado antes de tiempo por otro cliente, quien se traslada al Sur. Si quieres ver el local, llámanos esta tarde para concertar[4] una visita.

Saludos,

Dorothy Russell

1 Subjunctive after *para que* ....
2 *Locales*: 'premises'. The singular (*local*) is also frequent.
3 Literally, 'it gives to the street'.
4 Alternatives: *arreglar, acordar.*

42 Complaining about customs delay (fax)

To: HM Customs and Excise
London

From: Ordenasa, Madrid

Date: 21/2/9-

No. of pages: 1

Dear Sirs

On behalf of my director colleagues of this computer software business I wish to lodge a complaint about customs clearance at British airports.

On several occasions since October 199- materials freighted from Madrid to retailers in Great Britain have been subject to unexplained and unjustifiable delays. This company depends for success on its ability to respond quickly to market demand; furthermore, at all times the requisite export licences have been in order.

This communication by fax is prompted by the latest and most frustrating hold-up, at Gatwick Airport yesterday, which has allowed a market competitor to secure a valuable contract ahead of us.

If the Single Market is to function effectively, this is precisely the type of situation that must be avoided. I intend to contact the relevant Chamber of Commerce about this matter, but in the meantime I insist on an explanation from your officers as to why consignment AT/463 was not permitted immediate entry on 20 February 199-.

Yours faithfully

Dr. Norberto Mateos
(Managing Director)

42 Quejándose por el retraso en la Aduana (fax)

FAX

A: HM Customs and Excise
       Londres
De: Ordenasa, Madrid
Fecha: 21/2/9-
N°. de páginas: 1

Distinguidos Sres:

        En nombre de mis colegas, los directivos de esta empresa de software para ordenadores, deseo presentar queja[1] sobre el despacho de aduanas en los aeropuertos británicos.

En varias ocasiones, desde octubre de 199-, los materiales cargados en Madrid para los minoristas británicos han sido objeto de retrasos inexplicables e injustificados. El éxito de esta empresa depende de la rápida capacidad de respuesta a la demanda del mercado; además, los permisos indispensables para la exportación han estado, en todo momento, en regla.

Este fax es debido a la más reciente e inconcebible[2] retención, la de ayer en el aeropuerto de Gatwick, que tuvo como resultado que un competidor nuestro consiguiera un importante contrato antes que nosotros.

Si el Mercado Unico ha de[3] funcionar con eficacia, esta es precisamente la situación que debe evitarse. En lo que respecta a este asunto, pienso ponerme en contacto con la Cámara de Comercio pertinente, pero entretanto agradecería una explicación de parte de sus agentes de policía, en la que notificaran[4] por qué no le dieron entrada inmediata a la consignación AT/463 , el 20 de febrero 199-.

Les saluda atentamente,

                                Dr Norberto Mateos
                                    (Director)

1 Indefinite article (*una*) omitted.
2 'Frustrating' (see English letter) because inconceivable.
3 An alternative for future tense, with a hint of obligation.
4 Imperfect subjunctive: 'in which they notified (me) . . .'.

43 Stating delivery conditions

1 August 199-

Your Reference: JE/LR
Our Reference: TH/PA

Sr José Escalante
Managing Director
Escalante e hijos
Avenida del Sol
San Sebastián
SPAIN

Dear Mr Escalante

Thank you for your fax communication of yesterday regarding the delivery of the chickens and other poultry ordered by you from this company in early July. As we indicated in our original quote to Mr Salas, who first contacted us, the delivery can only be guaranteed if your bank is able to confirm that debts owed to us will be cleared this week.

Please note that our drivers would much appreciate assistance with overnight accommodation and that any costs they incur should be charged directly to Langley Farm once we have completed delivery next week.

We look forward to hearing from you on both matters.

Yours sincerely

Tom Holbrook
Transport Manager

43 Confirmando condiciones de entrega

Su Referencia: JE/LR
Nuestra Referencia: TH/PA

Sr José Escalante
Director Gerente
Escalante e hijos
Avenida del Sol
San Sebastián
España.   1.8.199-

Distinguido Sr Escalante:

Le agradecemos su comunicación por fax recibida ayer respecto al suministro de pollos y otras aves, pedido que usted hizo a esta empresa a principios de julio. Según le indicamos al Sr Salas en nuestro presupuesto original, cuando contactó con nosotros por primera vez, la entrega sólo puede ser garantizada si su banco nos confirma que las deudas a nuestro favor quedan[1] liquidadas esta semana.

Sírvase tomar nota de que[2] nuestros conductores[3] le agradecerían les prestara ayuda con el alojamiento de noche, y que cualquier gasto correrá a cargo de[4] Langley Farm una vez hayamos terminado la entrega la semana próxima.

Confiando en que pueda contestar a estos dos asuntos, le saluda atentamente.

T. Holbrook
(Jefe de Transportes)

1 *Quedar* can replace the verbs *ser* and *estar* in specific contexts (e.g. with past participles or other adjectives).
2 When verbs incorporating the word *de* (e.g. *acordarse de*) are followed by a subordinate clause, the *de* is retained and it precedes *que*, as in this case.
3 In Latin America the term *camioneros* is at least as commonly used.
4 *Correr a cargo de*: literally, 'to run to the charge of' ('to be the responsibility of').

44 Confirming time/place of delivery

12 June 199-

Your Reference: RCG/LP
Our Reference: FG/JD

Dr Rosa Castro Giménez
Subdirectora
Departamento de Relaciones Exteriores
Ministerio de Industria
Quito
ECUADOR

Dear Madam

Further to our communication of 9 May in which we outlined to your department the likely oil needs of the companies we represent, it is with some concern that we have heard indirectly that your Ministry may be unable to fulfil its immediate responsibilities. We would be most obliged to hear, at your earliest convenience, that the draft agreement signed recently by our representatives remains valid.

In spite of our concern we are fully committed to the trading relations discussed and as such wish to confirm details of first delivery of manufactured goods being exchanged for the above-mentioned oil imports. Carlton Excavators plc have confirmed this week that the consignment of earthmovers and tractors bound for Constructores Velasco was loaded on Monday of this week. It should reach the port of Guayaquil by the end of the month. We will, of course, provide you with more precise details nearer the time.

Meanwhile, please accept our best wishes for the continuation of our collaborative venture as we await your confirmation regarding the deliveries of your oil to the New South Wales terminal.

Yours faithfully

Frank Gardner
SENIOR PARTNER

44 Confirmando hora y lugar de entrega

Su Referencia: RCG/LP
Nuestra Referencia: FG/JD

Dra Rosa Castro Giménez
Subdirectora
Departamento de Relaciones Exteriores
Ministerio de Industria
Quito
Ecuador. 12.6.199-

Distinguida Sra:

Hacemos referencia a nuestra comunicación del 9 de mayo, en la que explicábamos a su Departamento las posibles necesidades de crudo que tienen las compañías que representamos. Nos preocupa el haber oído indirectamente que tal vez su Ministerio no pueda cumplir sus responsabilidades más inmediatas. Les quedaríamos muy agradecidos nos comunicaran, cuanto antes, si el acuerdo de proyecto[1] firmado recientemente por nuestros representantes es todavía válido.

A pesar de nuestra preocupación estamos enteramente comprometidos a las relaciones comerciales acordadas, y de ahí que les confirmamos datos sobre la primera entrega de mercancías manufacturadas a cambio de las importaciones de crudo a las que hemos hecho referencia antes. Excavadoras Carlton S.A. ha confirmado esta semana que la consignación de excavadoras y tractores dirigida a Constructores Velasco se cargó el lunes de la presente semana. Se espera que llegue al puerto de Guayaquil para finales de mes; huelga decir que[2] les pasaremos información detallada más cerca de la fecha.

Entretanto, confiando en que sabrán[3] aceptar la continua y mutua participación en esta colaboración, esperamos nos confirme la entrega del crudo a la terminal de New South Wales.

Le saluda con toda consideración.[4]

Frank Gardner
(Socio Mayoritario)

1 Alternatives: *de borrador*, (*acuerdo*) *preliminar*.
2 Idiomatic expression: 'it goes without saying that . . .'.
3 *Sabrán*: 'you will know how to' (adding formality).
4 Yet another variant of the final greeting.

45 Checking on mode of transportation

19 February 19-

Your ref. SM/MB
Our ref. TS/PU

Mr Sebastián Morán
Sales Manager
Hermanos García S.L.
Carretera Luis Viola, 24
CUENCA
Spain

Dear Mr Morán

Thank you for your letter sent on Tuesday last in which you refer to the kitchen equipment we ordered from García Brothers in December. As you know, our market has been rather depressed, although there are recent signs of improvement, and as a result we now need to receive the cupboard doors and worktops much more promptly than we had originally thought.

Can you please confirm that where necessary you would be able to deliver some items by road, or even by air if very urgent, rather than by the sea route you currently use?

We have checked that from Valencia it would be possible to airfreight at a reasonable price to East Midlands Airport on a Monday afternoon and a Thursday evening.

I would be grateful if you could send us a reply once you have been able to ascertain whether this proposal is viable.

Yours sincerely

Trevor Sharp
Warehouse Manager

45 Comprobando modo de transporte

Sr Sebastián Morán
Director de Ventas
Hermanos García S.L.
Carretera Luis Viola, 24
Cuenca
España.

Su ref. SM/MB
Nuestra ref. TS/PU

19.2.199-

Estimado Sr Morán:

Le agradezco su carta del pasado martes en la cual hace referencia al mobiliario de cocina que pedimos de Hermanos García en diciembre. Como saben, nuestro mercado ha estado en baja, aunque ya hay señales[1] de mejoría, y por consiguiente necesitamos recibir las puertas de los armarios y las encimeras mucho antes de lo que se ha solido pensar.[2]

¿Podría confirmar que si fuera[3] necesario nos entregarían alguna partida[4] por carretera, o incluso por avión si fuera muy urgente, en vez de hacer uso de la ruta marítima de costumbre?

Hemos comprobado que desde Valencia se podría hacer uso del transporte aéreo al aeropuerto de la Región Central Este, el lunes por la tarde y el jueves por la noche, a un precio razonable.

Le agradecería que, una vez haya averiguado si esta proposición es viable, nos envíe notificación.

Sin otro particular, le saluda atentamente

Trevor Sharp
(Jefe de Almacén)

1 Alternative: *indicios*.
2 Meaning: 'much earlier than we have tended to think'. *Soler*: 'to be accustomed to'.
3 *Fuera*, imperfect subjunctive: 'if/when it were . . .'.
4 *Partida*: 'batch, consignment'.

46 Claiming for transportation damage

24 January 199-

Claims Department
Lifeguard Assurance plc
Safeside House
High Street
Bromsgove
Worcs.

Dear Sir/Madam

POLICY NO. AL 78/2139B

My letter concerns a claim I wish to make on behalf of this firm, Anchor Lighting. We have had a policy with your company for many years, and rarely have needed to call upon your services. This time, however, we have suffered a serious financial loss due to damage incurred during the transit of goods.

Last week a whole consignment of lamps and other fittings was lost when our delivery truck ran off the road and turned over. The retail value of the merchandise ruined was in the region of £7,000, a sum equivalent to an entire quarter's profit.

I would be most grateful if you could send at your earliest convenience a major claim form and some general information on your settlement procedures.

Our policy number is as follows: AL 78/2139B.

I look forward to hearing from you soon.

Yours sincerely

Brian Tomkinson
(Proprietor)

46 Reclamando daños de transporte

Departamento de Daños y Reclamos
Seguros Salvavidas S.A.
Plaza Oriente
Valencia
España.   24.1.199-

Asunto: Póliza no. AL 78/2139B

Señor/Señora:

Por la presente hago referencia a una reclamación que deseo presentar en nombre de esta empresa, Balbica S.A. Estamos asegurados con ustedes desde hace muchos años, y en muy raras ocasiones hemos tenido que recurrir a ustedes. Ahora, sin embargo, hemos sufrido una gran pérdida financiera debido a daños incurridos en el transporte de mercancías.

La semana pasada una consignación completa de lámparas y otros accesorios fue totalmente destruida cuando nuestro camión de reparto se desbordó de la carretera y volcó. El valor al por menor[1] de las mercancías perdidas asciende a alrededor de 1.456.000 pesetas, suma equivalente a las ganancias totales de un trimestre.[2]

Le agradecería encarecidamente[3] nos enviara cuanto antes impreso de reclamación mayor, junto con información general sobre sus trámites[4] de pago.

El número de nuestra póliza es el siguiente: AL 78/2139B.

En espera de una pronta respuesta, le saluda atentamente

Bernardo Tomás
(Propietario)

1 Alternative: *al detalle*. (Wholesale: *al por mayor*).
2 Adjective: *trimestral*.
3 *Encarecer*: 'to beg' (formal).
4 Alternatives: *procedimiento, modo*.

47 Enquiring about customs clearance

5 November 199-

Your ref.
Our ref. TC/LJ

The Customs and Excise Branch
Foreign Ministry of Chile
SANTIAGO
Chile
South America

Dear Sirs

I have been advised to write to you directly by the Commercial Section of the Chilean Embassy in London. My company produces high-tech toys for the world market; at a recent trade fair in Barcelona several Chilean retailers expressed interest in importing our products, but were unable to provide information on customs formalities in your country. Similarly, the London Embassy has recommended that I consult your Branch to seek up-to-date information.

The situation is as follows: our products include computer games, remote-control toy cars, mini-sized televisions etc. It seems that goods made in the EC are subject to a customs process rather more restrictive than those from Japan or the USA. As my company is a wholly-owned subsidiary of a US parent firm, would it be easier and cheaper to export to Chile from the USA rather than from Britain?

My intention is not merely to circumvent regulations but to optimize our operations at a time when such matters as customs clearance can result in costly delays.

I thank you for your attention and look forward to an early reply.

Yours sincerely,

Thomas Carty
MANAGING DIRECTOR

47 Pidiendo información sobre mercancías pendientes de despacho en Aduana

Aduanas e Impuestos
Ministerio de Asuntos Exteriores
SANTIAGO
Chile.   5.11.199-

Nuestra ref. TC/LJ

Muy Sr mío:

El Departamento Comercial de la Embajada de Chile en Londres me ha aconsejado que me ponga directamente en contacto con usted.[1] Mi empresa se dedica a la fabricación de juguetes de alta tecnología para el mercado mundial; en una reciente feria comercial, que tuvo lugar en Barcelona, varios detallistas chilenos expresaron interés en importar nuestros productos, pero no pudieron informarnos acerca de las formalidades del despacho aduanero de su país. Asimismo, la Embajada en Londres me ha recomendado que consulte con su Sección, con objeto de ponerme al día.[2]

La situación es la siguiente: nuestros productos incluyen juegos para el ordenador, coches con mando a distancia, mini-televisores, etcétera. Parece ser que las mercancías fabricadas en la UE están sujetas a prácticas restrictivas aduaneras bastante más rígidas que las que se aplican al Japón y a los Estados Unidos. Debido a que mi empresa es una filial, propiedad por entero,[3] de una sociedad matriz[4] norteamericana ¿resultaría más fácil y más barato exportar a Chile desde los Estados Unidos que desde Gran Bretaña?

Mi propósito no es sólo salvar[5] el reglamento sino más bien optimizar nuestras operaciones en un momento en el que tales asuntos como el despacho de mercancías pendientes en Aduana pueden convertirse en un retraso costoso.

Le agradezco su colaboración, y en espera de una pronta respuesta le saludo atentamente,

Thomas Carty
(Director Gerente)

1 Referring to the unnamed official who will handle the matter.
2 Literally, 'put myself to the day'. Alternative: *actualizar(me)*.
3 A standard expression in commercial parlance.
4 From *matriz* (womb); meaning also 'headquarters of a company'.
5 Alternatives: *evitar, sortear*.

48 Undertaking customs formalities

27 November 199-

Your ref.
Our ref. AR/AP

HM Customs and Excise
Government Offices
LONDON WC2

Dear Sir/Madam

I write to inform you of a business operation in which my company is to be involved for the first time and to request your advice in the case of any misapprehension on my part.

As sole director of Leatherlux I have recently been able to conclude a deal with a firm of suppliers in Tunisia. I imagine that as a non-EU nation Tunisia cannot trade with complete freedom from import/export levies. I wish therefore to inform you that I intend to import from Nabeul in the next fortnight the following articles:

150 men's leather jackets
 50 pairs of ladies' leather trousers
250 leather belts
100 pairs of leather sandals
 50 pairs of men's leather boots

I anticipate paying approximately £3,000 for the consignment. Can you please provide me with official documentation (if required), or at least confirm, by fax if possible, that I shall be required to pay some form of duty on these imports?

I thank you in anticipation of your assistance.

Yours faithfully

Andrew Royston
Managing Director

48 Emprendiendo formalidades aduaneras

Sección de Aduanas
Ministerio de Asuntos Exteriores
Madrid.   27.11.199-

Nuestra ref. AR/AP

Distinguido/a Señor/Señora:

Le escribo con motivo de informarle sobre una operación comercial en la que mi empresa participará por vez primera,[1] y para que me asesoren[2] en caso de que esté equivocado.

Como director en exclusiva de Leatherlux, recientemente he concertado un trato con una empresa de abastecedores tunecinos. Supongo que, como Túnez no pertenece a la UE, no se le[3] permitirá comerciar sin estar sujeto a impuestos de importación y exportación. Por lo tanto, quisiera informarle que en la próxima quincena[4] tengo la intención de importar de Nabeul los artículos siguientes:

150 chaquetas de cuero[5] para caballero
 50 pares de pantalones de cuero para señora
250 cinturones de cuero
100 pares de sandalias de cuero
 50 pares de botas de cuero para caballero

Espero pagar aproximadamente 600.000 pesetas por la consignación. ¿Puede ser tan amable de[6] proporcionarme la documentación oficial (si ésta es necesaria) o por lo menos comunicarme por fax, si es posible, si tendré que pagar algún tipo de impuesto en estas importaciones?

Confiando en que pueda asistirme y agradeciéndole de antemano su información, le saluda muy atentamente,

Andrés Rodríguez
(Director Gerente)

1 A simple inversion: *por primera vez*.
2 Subjunctive after *para que*, expressing future intention.
3 The use of reflexive *se* and the indirect object pronoun (*le*) is typical of Spanish in rendering the passive ('will not be allowed to trade').
4 Literally, 'fifteen-day period'.
5 If it is soft leather (as in jackets/trousers), an equally appropriate word is *piel*.
6 'Please be so kind as to . . .'.

49 Informing of storage facilities

13 June 199-

Your ref. JG/TK
Our ref. JS/PI

Hurd's (International) Removals
34-36, Wesley Avenue
CROYDON
Surrey

Dear Mrs Gordon

I am pleased to inform you that the container of household goods your company contracted us to transport from Australia has now been delivered to our depot.

We will need by the end of this week to complete the official formalities, but you are welcome to pick up the unloaded contents for onward delivery to your customer from next Monday.

If you prefer to leave the goods here in store until further notice, please consult our price list (enclosed) which gives details of storage facilities and let us know your intention by fax.

As and when your driver does come to pick up the goods, he should enter the terminal by the side entrance which will lead him straight to the relevant loading area, marked DOMESTIC.

I trust these arrangements meet with your approval.

Yours sincerely

Jim Smith
Depot Manager

Enc.

49 Informando sobre facilidades de almacenamiento

Mudanzas Gómez
Zona Industrial Este
Alicante
España.   13.6.199-

Su ref. JG/TC
Nuestra ref. JS/PI

Estimada Sra Gómez:

Me complace informarle que el contenedor de artículos del hogar, para cuyo[1] transporte desde Australia nos contrató su compañía, ha sido entregado ahora en nuestro almacén aquí, en Barcelona.

Nos llevará[2] completar las formalidades oficiales hasta finales de semana, pero usted podrá pasar a recoger el contenido descargado, para que de esta forma pueda entregarlo a su cliente, a partir del lunes que viene.

Si prefiere dejar las mercancías aquí en almacén hasta previo aviso,[3] haga el favor de consultar la lista de precios (aquí incluida) que detalla las facilidades de almacenamiento, y sírvase comunicarme[4] por fax cuál es su intención.

Cuando su conductor venga a recoger las mercancías, debe de entrar en la terminal por la puerta lateral que le llevará directamente a la adecuada zona de carga señalada DOMÉSTICA.

En espera de que estas medidas[5] sean de su aprobación, e saluda cordialmente,

Juan Silvero
(Encargado de Almacén)

Anexo

1 *Cuyo*: 'whose' (i.e. the transportation).
2 *Llevar* in temporal expressions refers to length of time taken.
3 Literally, 'until prior warning'.
4 Note use of *me*: singular and plural freely interchanged in commercial correspondence.
5 'Measures'.

50 Assuring of confidentiality of information

1 November 199-

Your ref. EF/LJ
Our ref. HE/PI

Dr Ernesto Furillo
University Hospital
University of Managua
Managua
República de Nicaragua

Dear Dr Furillo

MISS ALICIA BARTOLOMÉ

Thank you for your letter of last month in which you sought confirmation that the reference you provided for Miss Alicia Bartolomé and her personal details would remain confidential.

It is the policy of the Government and of this Ministry to maintain total discretion when dealing with citizens from other countries who come to develop their professional studies. Miss Bartolomé's course begins in three weeks' time, by which time her curriculum vitae will have been duly stored on computer in this Ministry and will be accessible only to those with the due authorization.

As you will be well aware, the need for confidentiality in matters such as these is paramount, so you may rest assured that all proper measures will be taken to protect the interests of your institution and of its employees.

Yours sincerely

Hortensia Enríquez Castro
Personnel Supervisor

50 Asegurando confidencialidad en la información

Dr Ernesto Furillo
Hospital Universitario
Universidad de Managua
Managua
República de Nicaragua.

1.11.199-

Su ref. EF/LJ
Nuestra ref. HE/PI

Asunto: Srta Alicia Bartolomé

Distinguido Dr Furillo:

Le agradezco su carta del mes pasado en la[1] que solicitaba que la referencia y la información personal que usted proporcionó de la señorita Alicia Bartolomé se mantuvieran[2] confidenciales.

Tanto la política estatal como[3] la de este Ministerio es guardar discreción total cuando trata con ciudadanos de países extranjeros quienes vienen a ampliar sus estudios profesionales. El curso de la Srta Bartolomé dará comienzo dentro de tres semanas, y para entonces su currículum vitae[4] habrá sido archivado en la computadora de este Ministerio, al cual sólo tendrán acceso aquellas personas previamente[5] autorizadas.

Como usted bien sabe, es primordial mantener confidencialidad en asuntos de esta índole;[6] por lo tanto puede estar seguro que se tomarán todas las medidas adecuadas para proteger los intereses de su institución y del personal de la misma.

Me despido[7] con saludos cordiales.

Hortensia Enríquez Castro
(Supervisora de Personal)

1　The *la* is repeated in reference to *carta*.
2　Imperfect subjunctive after a past tense (*solicitaba*) in the main clause.
3　*Tanto ... como*: 'both'.
4　Frequently abbreviated to *currículum*.
5　Literally, 'previously'.
6　This word can be used to mean 'type', 'kind', 'nature'.
7　Literally, 'I say goodbye'.

51 Informing a client on conditions of loans/mortgages available

14 July 199-

Your ref. GB/LK
Our ref. EF/VE

Mr G Bernard
Managing Director
MultiCast
Floor 11
Forum House
Dukeries Avenue
Mansfield

Dear Mr Bernard

Since receiving your letter of 23 June we have been making enquiries on the matter of financing that you raised; please accept our apologies, nevertheless, for the delay. You will find enclosed three leaflets containing information about properties you may find interesting. We shall await your reaction to them.

More pressing, perhaps, is the question of finance. Having consulted local banks as well as our own finance broker, we have concluded that you would do best to arrange a meeting with the latter, Gilbert Cross, who will be pleased to outline for you in general terms a variety of mortgage as well as short-term loan plans.

All four major banks in town offer facilities for loans, so you may prefer to try them before or after meeting Mr Cross. However, it certainly appears that our broker can secure more favourable conditions if you are interested principally in a short-term loan.

Please contact our broker, whose address is below, about the kind of information you require:

Element Financial Services, Star Chambers, High Street, Worksop, Nottinghamshire.

Yours sincerely

Edward Fenton
Customer Liaison

Encs

51 Informando a un cliente sobre condiciones de préstamo/créditos hipotecarios

Sr G. Bernal
Director Gerente, Multivisión
Planta 11, Edificio Gil
Carrera 7/61
Bogotá, COLOMBIA.   14.7.199-

Su ref: GB/LK
Nuestra ref: EF/JU

Estimado Sr Bernal:

Desde que recibimos su carta del pasado 23 de junio hemos estado pidiendo informes sobre el asunto financiero al que usted se refería; no obstante, le pedimos nos disculpe por el retraso.

Le adjuntamos tres folletos que contienen información sobre inmuebles que pueden interesarle. Son muy fáciles de entender dichos folletos, y esperamos su comentario sobre los mismos.

Quizás[1] sea más urgente el asunto financiero. Habiendo consultado con los bancos locales, así como con nuestro agente financiero, llegamos a la conclusión de que sería mejor organizar una reunión con el Sr Gilberto Cruz, el cual[2] le explicará gustoso,[3] y en términos generales, la variedad de créditos hipotecarios, así como los planes de préstamo a corto plazo.

Los cuatro bancos principales de esta ciudad conceden facilidades de préstamo; por lo tanto quizá[1] usted prefiera consultar con ellos antes o después de la reunión con el Sr Cruz. No obstante, es casi seguro que nuestro agente financiero pueda conseguirle condiciones más favorables si usted está interesado principalmente en un préstamo a corto plazo.

Sírvase solicitar a nuestro agente, a la dirección abajo indicada, cualquier tipo de información que desee:

Asesoramiento[4] Financiero Cruz, Calle Medina 27, Lima, Perú.

Suyo atentamente

Eduardo Fuentes
(Servicio Clientes)

Anexos

1 Subjunctive form follows both variants of the word (*quizá/ás*).
2 Alternatives: *quien* or *que*; *el cual* is more specific.
3 Adjective replacing adverb (*gustosamente*).
4 'Advice', 'consultancy'.

52 Circulating local businesses with property services available

10 March 199-

Our ref. CE/MB

To: Directors of all businesses in the Castilla-León region

Dear Colleague

I take the opportunity to write to you on behalf of myself and my partner, Ana Martiarena, in order to publicize as widely as possible the property services we can make available to businesses in the region.

Since establishing our company here in 1976 we have gradually expanded our range of activities and clients. Most recently we have opened a free advice centre in Puentenorte for any member of the public to obtain up-to-date information on the property market.

As regards the needs of business, we offer the following services:

- a weekly guide to premises for rent and sale
- a direct link to sources of finance
- rent-collection service
- legal and insurance consultancy
- assistance in securing mortgages
- technical support in planning space and furbishment
- computer database linked to the national property network

These and many more services are available from us, and all are on your doorstep. Don't hesitate – call us today on 234 56 71 or come in person to 69 Calle Balbita, Puentenorte, where you can be sure of a warm welcome.

Yours sincerely

Carlos Estévez

52 Difundiendo información a empresas locales sobre servicios inmobiliarios

A: Los Sres Directores
    de todas las empresas
    de La Comunidad Autónoma de
    Castilla-León.   10.3.199-

Nuestra ref. CE/MB

Estimado colega:

En mi nombre, y en el de mi colega Ana Martiarena, le escribo para dar la máxima publicidad posible a los servicios inmobiliarios que tenemos disponibles a las pequeñas[1] empresas de esta Autonomía.

Desde que se estableció aquí nuestra compañía en 1976, hemos ido ampliando progresivamente nuestra gama de servicios y clientela; hace poco hemos inaugurado un consultorio gratuito en Puentenorte, cuyo objeto es poner al día al público en general sobre asuntos relacionados con el mercado inmobiliario.

Teniendo en cuenta[2] las necesidades de las empresas, ofrecemos los siguientes servicios:

- guía semanal de locales en alquiler y en venta
- contacto directo con fuentes financieras
- servicio de recaudación de renta
- asesoramiento legal y de seguros
- ayuda hipotecaria
- ayuda técnica en la planificación y renovación del espacio
- base de datos conectada a una red inmobiliaria nacional

Disponemos de esta y mucha más información, toda ella al alcance de su domicilio.[3] No lo dude,[4] llámenos[5] hoy al 234 56 71, o venga personalmente a la Calle Balbita 69, Puentenorte, donde le aseguramos una cordial bienvenida.

Le saluda muy atentamente,

                                          Carlos Estévez (Socio Superior)

1 Small and medium-sized businesses in Spain often are referred to collectively as PYMES: *Pequeñas y Medianas Empresas*.
2 *Tener en cuenta*: 'to take into account'.
3 'Your home'.
4 Literally, 'don't doubt it'.
5 Polite command to one person: 'call us'.

53 Advertising maintenance services available for office equipment

30 January 199-

Your ref.
Our ref. TC/JI

To: Office Managers:
Motor Sales businesses
in South London area

Dear Colleague

You may be aware from press advertising that the above firm offers a new service to the motor trade, particularly to maintain equipment used in processing stores supplies. Most large dealerships with service and accessories departments have installed a fully-integrated system that reduces drastically the need for large numbers of warehousemen.

The service charge is £350 per quarter, irrespective of visits made or problems solved; this figure also includes a component of insurance that covers both the dealership and ourselves against major breakdowns.

In recent months we have signed such service contracts with more than 40 dealerships whose names we are happy to supply if you are interested in checking our claims.

Thank you for your attention. Please do not hesitate to ring or fax us this week if the enclosed leaflet information is relevant to your needs.

Yours sincerely

Tom Cardinal
Managing Director

Enc.

53 Anunciando servicios de mantenimiento para equipos de oficina

Para: los directores administrativos de pequeñas empresas de venta de automóviles en el área del oeste de Barcelona.

Nuestra ref. TC/JI   30.1.199-

Estimado colega:

Tal vez[1] haya visto en los anuncios de la prensa que la empresa que figura en el membrete de esta carta ofrece un nuevo servicio a la industria del automóvil, especialmente con miras[2] a conservar en buen estado la maquinaria y el equipo utilizados[3] en el procesamiento de suministros de almacén.

La mayoría de las grandes concesiones[4] que disponen de departamento de servicio y de accesorios han[5] instalado un sistema completamente integrado que reduce drásticamente la necesidad de un gran número de almaceneros.

El coste del servicio es de 72.800 pesetas trimestrales,[6] sean cuantas sean[7] las visitas efectuadas o los problemas que se resuelvan; esta cantidad incluye asimismo un seguro que cubre tanto al concesionario[8] como a nosotros contra fallos importantes.

De pocos meses acá[9] hemos firmado tales contratos de servicio con más de cuarenta concesiones, cuyos nombres le facilitaremos gustosos si usted estuviera[10] interesado en comprobar nuestras declaraciones.

Le quedamos muy agradecidos por su atención y le rogamos no dude en telefonearnos o enviarnos un fax esta semana si la información especificada en el folleto adjunto está relacionada con sus necesidades.
Le saluda cordialmente

Tomás Cardenal
(Director Gerente)

Anexo

1 'Perhaps' (followed by subjunctive).
2 'With a view' (to).
3 Masculine plural adjective for feminine and masculine nouns.
4 *Concesiones*: 'franchized businesses', 'dealerships'.
5 Plural verb (*han instalado*) for (collective) singular subject.
6 'Quarterly' (adjective).
7 *Sean ... sean*: subjunctive, 'be they ... they might be'. The notion recurs in '*problemas ... resuelvan*', otherwise expressed.
8 Refers to the dealer (*concesionario*) who runs the franchise.
9 Literally, 'from few months (to) here', i.e. in recent months.
10 Imperfect subjunctive: 'if you were (interested)'.

113

54 Arranging a meeting for further discussions

5 November 199-

Our ref: TSS/EHK

Mr Angelo Ricasso
Cuscinetti SpA
Via Alessandro Manzoni, 32
20050 Triuggio (MI)
Italy

Dear Mr Ricasso

RE: THRUST BEARINGS

In 1989 we had discussions with you regarding the addition of our thrust bearings to the Dudley range for sale in your country.

We regret that due to many changes which have occurred in this company and in our parent company no progress was made with our arrangements, and we understand that it must have been disappointing for you not to have heard from us for such a long time.

We are now willing to try again, if you have not made other arrangements, and we would like to arrange a meeting with you at the Hardware Fair in Cologne next March.

We look forward to hearing from you,

Yours sincerely

Thomas Stone
SALES DIRECTOR

54 Concertando una reunión para tratar de un tema con más detalle

Nuestra Ref: TSS/EHK

Sr Angel Ricote
Ricote y Bermúdez S.A.
Zona Industrial No.3
Cartagena
España.

5.11.199-

Asunto: Cojinetes de empuje

Estimado Sr Ricote:

En 1989 tratamos con[1] usted acerca de incluir cojinetes de empuje a la gama Dudley, con objeto de venderlos en su país.

Debido a los numerosos cambios acaecidos[2] en esta empresa y en nuestra casa matriz, lamentamos informarle que no hemos progresado en nuestros acuerdos, y somos conscientes de que le habrá defraudado que no haya tenido noticias nuestras desde hace[3] tanto tiempo.

Ahora estamos dispuestos a intentarlo de nuevo, si usted no tiene otro compromiso,[4] y nos gustaría concertar una entrevista con usted en la Feria de Muestras de la Ferretería que se celebra en Colonia el próximo marzo.

En espera de sus prontas noticias, le saluda atentamente

Thomas Stone
(Director de Ventas)

1   *Tratar con*: 'to deal with'.
2   From *acaecer* (formal): 'to happen'.
3   Literally, 'since ago', used with present tense.
4   The same word can be used to mean: 'commitment', 'obligation', 'arrangement', 'agreement'.

55 Reservations

Enquiry about hotel accommodation (fax)

23 April 199-

Hotel Lucullus
Amadeusplatz 27
Hannover
Germany

Dear Sirs

I am attending the trade fair in Hanover in May with two colleagues, and we require rooms for three nights. Please could you confirm availability and price of the following:

three single rooms with bath/shower from 3 to 6 May.

Yours faithfully

Fred Garner

55 Reservas

Pidiendo información sobre alojamiento en un hotel (fax)

Hotel Lucrecia
Calle Mayor, 23
León
España.   23.4.199-

Estimados Sres:

Asistiré, junto con[1] otros dos colegas, a la Feria Comercial que se celebra en León en mayo y necesitamos alojamiento[2] para tres noches. Le ruego me comuniquen si tienen vacantes[3] y precios de:

tres habitaciones[4] individuales con baño/ducha[5] para los días del 3 al 6 de mayo.

Sin otro particular, le saluda cordialmente

Fred Garner

1   *Junto con*: '(along) with'.
2   'Accommodation', 'lodging(s)'.
3   *Vacante (la)*: 'vacancy' in hotel or company.
4   In much of Latin America *pieza* is preferred (in Mexico, *recámara*).
5   In Latin America bathroom facilities are described as *servicios*.

56 Reservations

Confirmation of reservation (fax)

30 October 199-

Ms G Cole
Ledington Parker plc
Moreton Avenue
Birmingham
B37 9KH

Dear Ms Cole

ROOM RESERVATION 15–18 NOVEMBER

We are pleased to confirm that we are able to offer the following accommodation for 15–18 November:

Four single rooms with shower/WC @ £150 per night, inclusive of breakfast and service.

We should be grateful if you could confirm the booking in writing as soon as possible.

Yours sincerely

H Japer
Manager

56 Reservas

Confirmando una reserva (fax)

Srta G Cole
Ledington Parker plc
Moreton Avenue
Birmingham
B37 9KH
Reino Unido.   30.10.199-

Asunto: Reserva[1] de habitaciones, 15–18 de noviembre

Estimada Srta Cole:

Nos complace confirmarle reserva de habitaciones del 15 al 18 de noviembre, y que[2] estamos gustosos de ofrecerle:

cuatro habitaciones individuales con ducha/WC al precio de 30,000 pesetas por noche, incluidos desayuno y servicio.

Le agradeceríamos confirmara por escrito,[3] y tan pronto le fuere[4] posible, dicha reserva.

Le saluda atentamente

E. Jabones (Sra)
Gerente

1   In Latin America, more frequently *reservación*.
2   The *que* follows from *Nos complace confirmarle*.
3   'In writing'.
4   A future subjunctive, rarely used except in documents or formal correspondence.

57 Reservations

Change of arrival date

11 March 199-

Ms J Hinton
Hotel Bonner
46 Southampton Way
London
SE39 8UH
England

Dear Madam

We have today received your confirmation of our booking of three single rooms from 18 to 23 March.

Unfortunately, we have had to change our plans, and shall not now arrive in London until the morning of 20 March. We would be grateful if you could change the reservation accordingly.

Yours faithfully

Henry Sands

57 Reservas

Cambio de la llegada al hotel

Srta J Hinton
Hotel Bonner
46 Southampton Way
London
SE39 8UH
Inglaterra.   11.3.199-

Estimada Srta:

Obra en nuestro poder[1] la confirmación de la reserva de tres habitaciones individuales para la fechas 18 a 23 de marzo.

Por desgracia, hemos tenido que cambiar de planes, y ahora no llegaremos a Londres hasta el 20 de marzo por la mañana. Le agradeceríamos cambiara dicha reserva tal y como sea posible.[2]

Sin otro particular, le saluda atentamente

Enrique Saenz

1   The use of this expression precludes reference to today as the time of receipt.
2   More literally, 'however it may be possible'; *tal (y) como* can be used with or without the link word.

58 Reservations

Request for confirmation of reservation

14 July 199-

Ms J Petersen
45 Dorrington Terrace
Bradford
Yorkshire
England

Dear Ms Petersen

You made a telephone reservation one week ago for a single room for two nights (20–22 July). We indicated to you when you made the reservation that we would hold it for one week, but that we required written confirmation.

If you still wish to reserve the room, could you please confirm by fax within 24 hours, or we shall have to reserve the room for other clients.

Thank you for your cooperation.

Yours sincerely

Victoria Palmer

58 Reservas

Pidiendo información sobre confirmación de una reserva

Srta J Petersen,
45 Dorrington Terrace
Bradford
Yorkshire
Inglaterra.   14.7.199-

Estimada Srta Petersen:

Hace una semana nos hizo una reserva, por teléfono, de una habitación individual para dos noches (20–22 de julio). Cuando habló con nosotros le dijimos que dicha reserva le quedaba hecha[1] para una semana, y que necesitábamos confirmación de la misma[2] por escrito.

Si todavía desea que dicha reserva sea en firme,[3] sírvase confirmárnoslo[4] por fax antes de veinticuatro horas, ya que de no ser así,[5] la reserva pasaría[6] a otro cliente.

Gracias por su cooperación y reciba un atento saludo

Victoria Palomar
(Secretaria)

1 Literally, 'remained made for you'.
2 The reservation.
3 *En firme*: 'firm(ly)'.
4 The *lo* refers to the client's desire to have a firm reservation.
5 *De no ser así*: 'if it is not the case'.
6 Conditional tense where future seems more logical.

59 Insurance

Request for quotation for fleet car insurance

1 July 199-

Hartson Insurance Services
24 Westbury Way
Sheffield
S12 9JF

Dear Sirs

We understand from colleagues that you specialize in insurance for company fleet cars. We have a large fleet of executive saloons, and are currently obtaining quotations for insurance cover.

If you are interested in giving us a quotation, could you please contact Ms Helen Bridges, our fleet manager, who will give you the appropriate details.

Yours faithfully

D J Spratt

59 Seguro

Solicitando presupuesto para asegurar flota de vehículos

Seguros López y Garrido
Calle de la Estación, 3–6
Pamplona
España.   1.7.199-

Muy señores nuestros:

Tenemos entendido, según colegas nuestros, que ustedes se especializan en los seguros de flotas de coches de empresa. La nuestra es una flota importante de turismos[1] para directivos y estamos solicitando actualmente presupuestos para asegurar dichos vehículos.

Si están interesados en ofrecernos su presupuesto, sírvase[2] ponerse en contacto con la señorita Elena Basuabla, encargada de nuestros vehículos, la cual le proveerá la información necesaria.

Les saluda atentamente

Diego Sebastián

1 'Saloon' is best rendered in Spanish as *turismo*, but it also implies a private car.
2 Note use of singular verb, immediately after plural in *están*.

60 Insurance

Reminder of overdue premium

2 June 199-

Mr R Collins
45 Delta Road
Stoke-on-Trent

Dear Mr Collins

Your vehicle, registration no. H351 AWL, is currently insured by us. We sent you several days ago a reminder that the insurance renewal premium was due. We have still not received this from you. We have to write to inform you that unless we receive payment within 72 hours, the insurance cover will lapse. Please send payment directly to our office in Gower Street, London.

Yours sincerely

Reginald Lawton
Customer Services

60 Seguro

Aviso de vencimiento de prima

Sr R. Collar
Comunicaciones A1
Calle 2 de Agosto, 65
San Sebastián
España.   2.6.199-

Estimado Sr Collar:

       Hacemos referencia a su vehículo, matrícula Nº. H351 AWL,
que tiene asegurado con nosotros. Hace varios días le enviamos aviso de
renovación de prima[1], pero todavía no hemos recibido pago de la misma. Nos
ponemos en contacto con usted para informarle que, de no recibir dicho pago[2]
en un período de, a más tardar, setenta y dos horas, daremos por anulado[3] el
seguro de cobertura.[4] Sírvase enviar pago directamente a nuestras oficinas de la
Calle Gower, en Londres.

Le saluda atentamente

Reginald Lawton
(Servicios al cliente)

1 Alternatively, *notificación de renovación de prima*.
2 Payment of the new premium.
3 *Dar por anulado*: 'to take as cancelled'.
4 'Cover(age)' of all kinds.

61 Insurance

Submission of documents to support claim

4 April 199-

Darton Insurance Services
59 Tristan Road
Uttoxeter
Staffordshire

Dear Sirs

I submitted to you several days ago a claim form under the terms of my motor vehicle insurance (policy number CDF 9486756 UY 94766). Your head office has since requested from me the original policy document. I regret that this is no longer in my possession, and I enclose herewith a photocopy. I trust that this will meet your requirements.

Yours faithfully

A Lightowlers

Enc.

61 Seguro

Presentando documentos para apoyar una reclamación

Asprilla y Rincón Cía. de Seguros
Edificio Monumental
Plaza de los Reyes
Madrid.   4 de abril, 199-

Muy señores míos:

Hace varios días les presenté un impreso de reclamación según las condiciones de seguro de mi vehículo (póliza N° CDF 9486756 UY 94766). Ahora la oficina central de su empresa me ha pedido el documento original de dicha póliza. Lamento informarles que éste ya no obra en mi poder, y por lo tanto les adjunto una fotocopia del mismo,[1] que espero sea admisible.[2]

Atentamente les saluda

Alejandro Latilla

Anexo

1 Referring to the policy document.
2 Also acceptable: *adecuado*.

62   Insurance

Taking out third party vehicle insurance

11 October 199-

Uxbridge Insurance
Grosvenor House
12b Weston Terrace
Bournemouth
Hants

Dear Sirs

RE: QUOTATION RC28FO

With reference to the above quotation, I confirm that I wish to take out Third Party car insurance, and enclose the appropriate fee in the form of a cheque.

I should be grateful if you could send me confirmation and the policy certificate as soon as possible.

Yours faithfully

Julie Vincent

62 Seguro

Seguro de vehículo a terceros

Uxbridge Insurance
Grosvenor House
12b Weston Terrace
Bournemouth
Hants.
Inglaterra.   el once de octubre de 199-

Asunto: Presupuesto Nº RC28FO

Estimados señores:

De acuerdo con[1] el presupuesto recibido, les comunico que desearía asegurar mi vehículo a terceros,[2] por lo que adjunto, a tales efectos,[3] cheque por valor de la cantidad presupuestada.

Les agradecería me notificaran recibo[4] de dicho cheque y me enviasen asimismo la póliza lo antes posible.

Sin otro particular, les saluda atentamente

Julia Venegas

Anexo

1 Literally, 'in accordance with'.
2 Fully comprehensive (as opposed to third party, *a terceros*) would be: *contra todo riesgo*.
3 Formal: 'for this purpose'.
4 'Receipt': in this case not the document, but the act of receiving.

63 Insurance

Refusal to meet claim

9 April 199-

Ms D Leach
29 Janison Avenue
York

Dear Ms Leach

RE: CLAIM NO. JH 8576/HY

We acknowledge receipt of your claim form (reference JH 8576/HY) concerning water damage to your stock on the night of 27 March. We regret, however, that we are unable to meet the claim, as our policy (section 3, paragraph 5) specifically excludes this form of damage, particularly since the premises were unoccupied for a period of two weeks before the damage occurred.

Yours sincerely

Peter Ardley

63 Seguro

Negándose a saldar un reclamo

Srta L. Vicario
Prendas Sporty
Centro Comercial El Yate
Gerona
España.   9.4.199-

Asunto: Reclamación JH 8576/HY

Estimada señorita Vicario:

Acusamos recibo de su reclamación (referencia JH 8576/HY) concerniente a los daños que el agua ocasionó a sus existencias en la noche del pasado[1] 27 de marzo. Sentimos informarle que no podemos abonarle[2] el pago de dicha reclamación, ya que la sección 3, apartado 5, de dicha póliza excluye este tipo de daño, debido especialmente a que los locales estuvieran[3] vacíos durante dos semanas antes de haber ocurrido los daños.

Le saluda muy atentamente

                                                                                    Pedro Ardiles

1   When referring to dates in the recent past this (redundant) term is frequently included in correspondence.
2   *Abonar*: 'to credit', 'pay out'.
3   Also *estuvieron* (indicative past tense); the use of imperfect subjunctive can be determined by the preceding *debido a que*.

64 Considering legal action

24 May 199-

Cabinet Rossignol
4 rue des Glaïeuls
75009 Paris
France

For the attention of Maître Patelin

Dear Maître Patelin

Your name was given to us by Robert Mackenzie of Canine Crunch Ltd for whom you acted last year.

We have a complaint against the newspaper *La Gazette du Samedi* who have, in our opinion, seriously defamed us in the enclosed article dealing with the closure of our plant at Roissy-en-France.

We would wish to take legal action against the said journal but before taking this step would like to have your professional advice on the strength of our case. Could you also, at the same time, let us know how long such a case might run and the likely scale of our legal costs.

Yours sincerely

Lionel E Bone
Managing Director

Enc.

64 Asesoramiento legal: daños

Cabinet Rossignol
4 rue des Glaïeuls
75009 París
Francia.   24 de mayo de 199-

Para la atención del Maître Patelin

Estimado Señor Patelin:

Su nombre nos fue proporcionado[1] por el señor Rodrigo
Mendoza de Hermanos Ibarra, a quien usted representó el año pasado.

Deseamos presentar una queja[2] contra el diario *La Gazette du Samedi*, que en
nuestra opinión nos ha calumniado gravemente en el artículo que le adjunto, y
que se trata del cierre de nuestra fábrica de Roissy-en-France.

Quisiéramos entablar demanda[3] contra el mencionado diario, pero antes de
proceder a ello[4] nos gustaría nos proporcionara asesoramiento jurídico sobre el
peso de nuestro caso. Asimismo, le agradeceríamos nos notificara la posible
duración del mismo[5] y a lo que pueden subir los honorarios jurídicos.

Le saluda muy atentamente

Leonardo Duarte
Director Gerente

Anexo

1   *Proporcionar*: 'to provide', 'supply'. (See also below *nos gustaría nos proporcionara*: 'we
    would like that you should provide').
2   The standard expression for lodging of complaints.
3   Alternatives: *demandar a, llevar a juicio*.
4   *Ello*: i.e., the bringing of the lawsuit.
5   'The case in question'.

65 Requesting information on setting up a plant abroad

23 May 199-

Office Notarial
84 rue du Grand Pineau
85000 Olonnes sur Mer
France

Dear Sirs

Our company is proposing to set up a dairy produce processing plant in western France and we would like you to find us a suitable site.

We need either freehold or leasehold premises of 2,000 square metres on a plot with easy access for large vehicles.

Can you help us in finding the site and act for us in its acquisition? This is our first venture into France so we would appreciate all additional information about property purchase or leasing.

Yours faithfully

Arthur Sturrock
Managing Director

65 Asesoramiento legal: compra de bienes en el extranjero

Hernández y socios
Calle Luis de León, 76
Salamanca
España.   23 de mayo de 199-

Muy Sres míos:

        Nuestra empresa se propone instalar una fábrica para la elaboración de productos lácteos en el oeste de España, y nos gustaría encargarles[1] a ustedes que nos buscaran[2] un lugar adecuado.

Necesitamos disponer de una nave[3] de dos mil metros cuadrados con fácil acceso para vehículos de gran tonelaje, bien sea[4] de adquisición absoluta[5] o para arrendar.[6]

¿Podrían ustedes buscarnos un solar y representarnos en la adquisición del mismo? Este es nuestro primer negocio en España, y por lo tanto les agradeceríamos todo tipo de información adicional sobre compra o alquiler de propiedades.

Aprovecho[7] gustoso para saludarles atentamente.

Arthur Sturrock
Director Gerente

1 *Encargar*: 'to entrust'.
2 Imperfect subjunctive after conditional form in main clause.
3 Technical term: 'premises' (e.g. *nave industrial*). The word can also mean 'ship'.
4 *Bien sea*: 'whether it be'.
5 'Outright purchase'.
6 'To rent'.
7 *Aprovechar*: 'to take advantage', 'take the opportunity'.

66 Complaint about delay in administering a bank account

8 September 199-

Société Bancaire Générale
4 boulevard Leclerc
76200 Dieppe
France

<u>For the attention of the Manager</u>

Dear Sir

<u>RE: ACCOUNT NO. 654231</u>

We have received the July statement of our above account no. 654231 and are surprised that the balance shown is so low.

We have been assured by two of our major customers, Alligand SA and Berthaud Etains, that they settled large outstanding invoices by bank transfer to that account four weeks and five weeks ago respectively.

Will you please check very carefully and let us know by fax the exact balance of our account. If, as we think, work is being processed by you in a dilatory fashion, please could you let us know the reason for this.

Yours sincerely

Eric Smith
Finance Director

66 Queja sobre demora en la gestión de una cuenta bancaria

Banco Mediterráneo
Calle Calderón, 67
Reus
España.   8 de setiembre de 199-

Para la atención del Sr Director

Asunto: cuenta No. 654231

Muy Sr mío:

Hemos recibido el estado[1] de nuestra cuenta (No. 654231) perteneciente al mes de julio, y nos sorprende saber que el balance sea[2] tan bajo.

Dos de nuestros importantes clientes, Alimate S.A. y Bernabeu Martín, nos aseguran que han saldado[3] las facturas importantes que tenían pendientes por medio de transferencia bancaria a dicha cuenta, hace cuatro y cinco semanas respectivamente.

Sírvase revisar meticulosamente el balance exacto de nuestra cuenta, y envíenoslo[4] por fax. Si, como pensamos, usted va retrasado en esta gestión,[5] tenga a bien comunicarnos la razón de ello.

Atentamente,

Eric Smith
Director de Finanzas

1 *Balance* might also be used here, if it were not to be quoted just after with the more specific meaning of 'cash in credit'.
2 Subjunctive after a verb of emotion (surprise).
3 Alternatives: *liquidar, pagar.*
4 An *usted* command: 'send it to us'.
5 'Action', 'running', 'procedure'.

67 Complaint about mail delivery

19 November 199-

The Central Post Office
Place Centrale
53000 Laval
France

Dear Sirs

We have made some enquiries here in England concerning delays we have experienced in the delivery of our mail to our subsidiary in Cossé le Vivien and have been informed that these are being caused at the Laval sorting office.

Since our business is being seriously inconvenienced by postal delays we would be most grateful if you could look into the matter.

It should not take 10 days for orders and invoices to get from us to our colleagues in Cossé. We therefore enclose a sample mailing on which the dates are clearly marked.

Yours faithfully

Jeremy P Johnson
Director

Enc.

67 Queja sobre reparto de correo

Le Bureau de Poste
Place Centrale
53000 Laval
Francia.   19 de noviembre de 199-

Señores:

Les notificamos que hemos pedido información aquí en España
acerca de los retrasos existentes en el despacho del correo a nuestra filial en
Cossé le Vivien, y nos comunican que las causas de éstos[1] corresponden a[2] la
oficina de distribución del correo de Laval.

Puesto que los retrasos postales están causando grandes inconvenientes a
nuestro negocio, les agradeceríamos investigaran este asunto.

Los pedidos y las facturas que circulan entre nosotros y nuestros colegas de
Cossé no deberían tardar diez días; de ahí que[3] les remitimos[4] una muestra de
correo en la cual figura, con toda claridad, la fecha del matasellos.[5]

Sin otro particular, les saludamos atentamente

                                                    María José Forlán (Srta)
                                                    Directora

Anexo

1 The delays.
2 *Corresponder a*: 'to relate to', 'concern'.
3 Literally, 'hence'.
4 *Remitir*: 'to send' (of mail, in particular).
5 'Postmark', 'date stamp'.

68 Complaint about wrong consignment of goods

1 September 199-

Dessous Dessus
14 rue Legrand
80000 Amiens
France

For the attention of Mr A Malraux

Dear Mr Malraux

RE: INVOICE NO. 13322/08/92

We regret to inform you that the garments you sent us in your consignment of 25 August were not what we had ordered.

Please refer to our order (copy enclosed) and to your invoice (no. 13322/08/92). You will note that the briefs, slips and bras are mostly the wrong sizes, colours and materials.

We are at a loss to explain this departure from your normally reliable service. Will you please contact us immediately so that we can put matters right?

Yours sincerely

Fred Smith
Manager

Enc.

68 Queja sobre entrega errónea de mercancías

Vestisa
Polígono Industrial El León
Sabadell
España.

1 de setiembre de 199-

Para la atención del Sr A. Maldonado

Asunto: Pedido N° 13322/08/92

Estimado Sr Maldonado:

Lamentamos informarle que las prendas que nos envió en la remesa del 25 de agosto no eran las que habíamos pedido.

Sírvase hacer referencia a nuestro pedido (cuya copia le adjuntamos) y a su factura (no. 13322/08/92). Comprobará[1] que las bragas, las enaguas y los sujetadores, en su mayoría, no corresponden ni[2] en las tallas, ni en los colores , ni en la composición del tejido.

Nos sorprende la alteración[3] de este servicio hasta ahora digno de crédito.[4] Le agradeceríamos se pusiera en contacto con nosotros inmediatamente, con objeto de resolver este asunto.

Atentos saludos

Fred Smith
Gerente

Anexo

1 *Comprobar*: 'to check'. Alternatives: *verificar, revisar; chequear* in parts of Latin America.
2 *Ni . . . ni . . . ni . . .*: neither, nor, nor.
3 Alternatives: *cambio, modificación* (deliberate); *alteración* here is unlikely to imply an intentional change in practice.
4 Formal: 'worthy of credit', 'creditable'.

69 Complaint about damage to goods

3 April 199-

Transports Transmanche SA
Quai des Brumes
14000 Caen
France

For the attention of Mr Gérard Dispendieux

Dear Monsieur Dispendieux

We have received a complaint from John Ferguson of Amex Insurance concerning his company's removal to Beauvais three weeks ago. You will remember that we subcontracted this removal to your company.

Mr Ferguson claims that several of the items of furniture and office equipment were damaged on arrival at the premises in Beauvais.

Although he complained there and then to your deliverymen, he has still not heard from you. In the interests of our future business relations I would be grateful if you could clarify this situation.

Yours sincerely

Gerald Wagstaffe
French Area Manager

69 Queja sobre artículos dañados

Mudanzas Garranzo
Bulevar Las Hayas, 35
Badajoz
España.

3 de abril de 199-

Para la atención del Sr Jorge Deva

Estimado Sr Deva:

Hemos recibido una queja del señor John Ferguson, de Seguros Amex, concerniente al[1] traslado de su firma[2] a Badajoz hace tres semanas. Si recuerda, subcontratamos a su empresa para efectuar dicha mudanza.[3]

El Sr Ferguson afirma que algunos de los muebles y enseres de oficina estaban estropeados a su llegada al local de Badajoz.

A pesar de que el Sr Ferguson se quejó a los transportistas en el acto,[4] usted todavía no se ha puesto en contacto con él. En beneficio de seguir, en el futuro, la buena relación entre ambas compañías, le agradecería aclarara esta situación.

Le saluda atentamente

Gerald Wagstaffe
Gerente de la Zona Española

1 Alternatives: *relativo a, relacionado con, en cuanto a, en lo que se refiere a, respecto a.*
2 It is the firm, rather than just Mr Ferguson, that has moved.
3 *Mudanza* is more specifically the removal of goods on a fairly permanent basis; *traslado* can apply simply to the transfer of personnel.
4 Literally, 'on the spot'.

70 Informing customers that a company has been taken over

24 July 199-

Produits Chimiques SA
89 rue Jules Barni
80330 Longueau
France

Dear Sirs

Thank you for your order dated 17 July. We have to inform you, however, that our company has been taken over by a larger concern, INTERNATIONAL CHEMICALS Inc.

As a result of this, we have to tell you that we no longer produce the polymers that you request at this site. We have, however, passed on your order to our parent company and are confident that you will be contacted soon.

In the interests of our future business relations we enclose the latest catalogue of our total range of products, indicating which subsidiary manufactures which product.

Yours faithfully

Frederick Herriot
Plant Director

Enc.

70 Informando sobre cambios en una empresa: adquisición

Químicos Vascos S.A.
Zona Industrial de Andoaín
País Vasco
España.   24 de julio de 199-

Muy Sres nuestros:

    Les agradecemos su pedido fecha[1] 17 de los corrientes.[2] Debemos informarles no obstante, que una empresa mayor, Químicos Internacionales S.A., ha absorbido la nuestra.[3]

Además de ello,[4] les comunicamos que en este lugar ya no fabricamos los polímeros que ustedes piden. Sin embargo, hemos enviado el pedido a nuestra empresa matriz y confiamos que se pondrán en contacto con ustedes en breve.

En beneficio de seguir manteniendo futuras relaciones comerciales, adjuntamos el último catálogo que ilustra la gama completa de nuestros productos, así como[5] el nombre de las filiales y el nombre de los productos que fabrica cada una de ellas.

Sin otro particular, les saludamos atentamente.

Frederick Herriot
Director de Fábrica

Anexo

1 Omission of *de* or *con* before the key word (*fecha*) is normal in commercial correspondence.
2 Because the month of July appears in the heading, this term (meaning 'the current days') can be used in reference to 17 July, and is typical in this context.
3 *La nuestra*: 'ours' (company).
4 *Ello*: 'all the above-mentioned information' ('it').
5 Literally, 'thus as' ('as well as').

71 Informing customers of change of name and address

EUROPEAN COMMERCIAL INSURANCE Ltd
47 Broad Walk
Preston
Lancashire United Kingdom

(Formerly PRESTON INSURERS Inkerman Street, Preston)

1 June 199-

The Export Manager
Nouveaux Textiles
342 chaussée Baron
59100 Roubaix
France

Dear Sir

RE: CHANGE OF COMPANY NAME AND ADDRESS

We are writing to all our valued customers to inform them that Preston Insurers has changed both its registered name and its address.

We are still located in Preston and operating as commercial insurers as before. However, we have acquired new partners who have invested fresh capital in the business.

It is our intention to increase our European business, hence the new name. Enclosed is our brochure setting out our range of services and tariffs. Do not hesitate to contact us if you have any queries about these changes.

Yours faithfully

Nancy Wilton
Customer Liaison Manager

Enc.

71 Informando sobre cambio de nombre y dirección de una empresa

European Commercial Insurance Ltd
(Formerly Preston Insurers, Inkerman Street, Preston)
47 Broad Walk
Preston
Lancashire
Reino Unido.
Tel. +44 772 345217
Fax +44 772 345192

La Directora Gerente
Cosmética Ayala de Ruch
Paseo de la Concha, 12
Santander
España.   1 de junio de 199-

Asunto: Cambio de nombre de empresa y de dirección

Estimada señora:

Por la presente[1] notificamos a todos nuestros estimados clientes que hemos cambiado de nombre comercial y de dirección.

Todavía seguimos ubicados en Preston y, como antes, seguimos dedicándonos a los seguros comerciales. Sin embargo, hemos adquirido a socios nuevos que han invertido capital en el negocio.

Tenemos pensado expansionar nuestros negocios con Europa y de ahí que haya surgido[2] el nuevo nombre. Adjunto le enviamos nuestro catálogo en el que figura nuestra gama de servicios y precios. Si tiene alguna duda sobre estos cambios, no deje de[3] contactar con nosotros.

Cordialmente le saluda

                                                              Nancy Wilton
                                              Encargada de Relaciones Públicas

Anexo

1 Formal: 'by the present (letter)', 'in writing'.
2 *Surgir*: 'to spring', 'derive'. Alternatives: *provenir, originar.*
3 *Dejar de*: 'to omit to', 'fail to'. In this case, a polite command.

72 Informing customers of increased prices

12 November 199-

Epicerie Fine
9 rue Dutour
72100 Le Mans
France

Dear Monsieur Olivier

In reply to your letter of the 5th I am sending you a new price list.

You will note that all of our prices have increased by some 6.3 per cent. This was unfortunately made necessary by our continuing inflation as well as the British Chancellor's recent decision to increase the general rate of VAT to 17.5 per cent.

I hope that the quality of our produce will continue to engage your loyalty. It is also the case that the pound sterling has reduced in value – thanks to the Chancellor!

Yours sincerely

Michael McDermott
Marketing Manager

Enc.

72 Informando sobre cambios de precios

AliDeliSA
Calle de la Fuente, 45–47
La Coruña
España.   12 de noviembre de 199-

Distinguidos Señores:

En contestación a su carta del cinco de los corrientes, adjunto remito[1] la nueva lista de precios.

Observará que todos nuestros precios han aumentado en un 6,3%.[2] Este aumento ha sido debido tanto a la continua inflación como a la reciente decisión tomada por nuestro Ministro de Hacienda de aumentar al 17,5% el tipo[3] de interés general del IVA.

Espero que la calidad de nuestros productos alimenticios continúe siendo de su agrado.[4] También se da el caso de[5] que la libra esterlina ha disminuido de valor. ¡Le daré las gracias de su parte al Ministro de Hacienda!

Sin otro particular, aprovecho para saludarle gustoso.

Michael McDermott
Director de Márketing

Anexo

1 Literally, 'I send attached'.
2 Note comma rather than full point in decimal figure. Percentage references are preceded in Spanish by *en* or *por*.
3 In Latin America *tasa* is preferred to *tipo*.
4 The Spanish is simplified from the slightly ironic English.
5 *Darse el caso* (*de*): 'to arise', 'come about'.

73 Requesting information about opening a business account

23 October 199-

The Manager
Crédit Mercantile
89 rue Béranger
69631 VÉNISSIEUX
France

Dear Sir

We are proposing to open an office and refrigerated storage facility at Vénissieux in the new year and would appreciate it if you would send us some information about opening a bank account at your branch.

Initially we would be transferring funds to finance the setting up of our new business premises. Thereafter we would expect to use the account to receive payments from French customers and to pay local suppliers etc.

We would be most grateful if you could inform us of all the formalities that we need to observe, both public and particular, to Crédit Mercantile. Could you also inform us of your charges on business accounts?

Yours faithfully

Alfred Sanger
Commercial Manager

73 Solicitando información sobre la apertura de cuenta bancaria de negocios

El Director
Banque de Crédit Mercantile
89 rue Béranger
69631 Vénissieux
Francia.   23 de octubre de 199-

Muy señor nuestro:

A primeros del año que viene[1] nos proponemos abrir una oficina y un depósito de almacenaje refrigerado en Vénissieux, por lo que les agradeceríamos nos enviaran información sobre la apertura de una cuenta bancaria en su sucursal.[2]

En principio trasladaríamos fondos para financiar la puesta en marcha de un nuevo local comercial; luego haríamos uso de dicha cuenta para que nuestros clientes franceses nos abonaran pagos a nuestro favor y para efectuar[3] pagos a los abastecedores locales etcétera.

Le agradeceríamos encarecidamente nos informaran de todas las formalidades que debemos cumplir, tanto las públicas como las que correspondan al Banque de Crédit Mercantile. Asimismo sírvase informarnos de los gastos bancarios cobrados a empresas.

Sin otro particular, aprovechamos esta ocasión para saludarle atentamente.

Alfonso Sabio
Director Comercial

---

1 Alternatives: *año nuevo, año próximo.*
2 *Agencia* can also be used.
3 Infinitive here (cf. *abonaran*) because continuation of main clause.

74 Requesting information about opening a personal bank account

4 November 199-

The Manager
Banque Nationale
146 boulevard Haussmann
75016 Paris
France

Dear Sir

My British employers are posting me to their French subsidiary as of the beginning of next January. I will therefore be moving to Paris with my family and I expect to be resident in France for two years.

Will you please send me information about opening a personal current account at your bank? My salary would be paid into the account and both my wife and I would wish to draw money from it and to pay bills by cheque etc. We may also wish to transfer money to a bank account in England.

Please send me any documentation you have. By the way, I *can* read French though I am not very good at writing it.

Thank you in advance for your assistance.

Yours faithfully

Stuart Smith

74 Solicitando información sobre apertura de cuenta corriente

El Director
Banque Nationale
146 boulevard Haussmann
75016 París
Francia.   4 de noviembre de 199-

Muy señor mío:

A primeros de enero próximo mi compañía va a trasladarme de España a la filial francesa. Por lo tanto me voy a mudar[1] a París con mi familia, y espero fijar[2] mi residencia en Francia por dos años.

Sírvase enviarme información sobre apertura de cuenta corriente personal en su banco. Mi sueldo se abonará directamente en la cuenta; tanto mi esposa como yo retiraríamos fondos de ella y abonaríamos facturas por medio de cheque bancario etcétera. Es probable que también queramos[3] transferir dinero a una cuenta bancaria en España.

Le agradecería me enviara la información pertinente. Nótese[4] que leo el francés, aunque no lo escribo muy bien.

Reiterándole las gracias anticipadas,[5] le saluda atentamente

                                          Sergio Castro Escudero

1 *Mudarse* (*de casa*): 'to move' (house).
2 *Fijar la residencia*: 'to take up (permanent) residence'.
3 Subjunctive after '*Es probable que* . . .'.
4 A polite/formal reminder to the bank manager.
5 'Thanks in advance', with repetition implied.

75 Letter re overdrawn account

9 March 199-

J H Jameson
47 Narrow Bank
Lichfield
Staffordshire

Dear Mr Jameson

We regret to inform you that your account, number 62467840, is overdrawn by £21.09.

We would appreciate your rectifying this situation as soon as possible, since you have no overdraft arrangement with us.

Yours sincerely

F E Jones
Manager

75 Carta en relación con estado de cuenta en números rojos[1]

Sr Alberto Ferrer
Calle Contreras, 27 4, izq.[2]
San Sebastián
País Vasco
España.   9 de marzo de 199-

Distinguido[3] Sr Ferrer:

Lamentamos informarle que su cuenta No. 62467840 arroja un saldo[4] de veintiuna libras esterlinas con nueve peniques, cantidad a nuestro favor.[5]

Le agradeceríamos rectificara esta situación lo antes posible, ya que usted no dispone de acuerdo con nosotros a este respecto.[6]

Le saluda atentamente,

                                                             F E Jones
                                                             Director

1   Literally, 'in the red'.
2   4th floor, on the left. Presumably there are only two apartments on this floor (to the right and to the left).
3   A rather complimentary form of address in view of the nature of the letter.
4   Literally, 'throws up a balance'.
5   *Cantidad a nuestro favor*: 'debit balance'. See also *saldo deudor/negativo*: 'debit balance'.
6   I.e. regarding overdrafts.

76 Informing a customer of a bank deposit

2 May 199–

Mr Bernard J Mann
4 Beauchamp Mews
London
England

Dear Mr Mann

We are writing to inform you that we have today received a cheque payable to you for the sum of $124,035.00 and sent by J et P Barraud Notaires, 307 rue du Château, Luxembourg.

Can you please confirm as soon as possible whether you were expecting this deposit and let us know your instructions concerning it?

Enclosed is a photocopy of this cheque and its accompanying letter.

Yours sincerely

Amélia Dupont
Head Cashier

Encs

76 Notificando al cliente sobre transferencia a su favor

Sr Arturo Pérez
Impex S.L.
Calle Dolores Butraga, 87
Lugo
España.   2 de mayo de 199-

Distinguido Sr Pérez:

Nos es grato comunicarle que hoy hemos recibido un cheque a su favor, por la cantidad de 124.035 dólares, enviado por los notarios J. y P. Barraud de Rue du Château 307, Luxemburgo.

Sírvase confirmar, lo antes posible, si usted tenía previa notificación[1] de que dicho cheque iba a ser abonado aquí, y sus instrucciones a este respecto.

Adjunto[2] envío fotocopia del cheque y de la carta que acompañaba al mismo.

Sin otro particular, y en espera de sus instrucciones,[3] le saluda

Amélie Dupont
Cajera en jefe

Anexos

1   Literally, 'prior notification'.
2   Here used as an adverb; 'I send enclosed . . .'.
3   A typical, if gratuitous, inclusion here.

77   Enquiry about banking

Letter from the Ombudsman

4 April 199-

Monsieur J. Delor
Président-Directeur Général
Mouton-Poulenc
7 rue du Trocadéro
Paris 3 Cedex
France

Dear Sir

In response to your general query about banking in England, there are two main types of bank, merchant banks and commercial banks. The former are very numerous and deal with companies generally. The latter are mainly the four big groups: Lloyds, National Westminster, Barclays and Midland.

The enclosed leaflet will give you further details, including information about banking in Scotland. Our office is mainly concerned with complaints about banks.

In addition you should note that The Post Office also has some banking and money transfer facilities.

Yours faithfully

C D Prettyman
For the Ombudsman

Enc.

77 Solicitando información sobre la banca

Carta del Defensor

Dr Alonso Torrete
Apartado Aéreo 341[1]
Buenos Aires
República de Argentina.

4 de abril de 199-

Distinguido Doctor:

Doy contestación a la duda general que tiene usted sobre la banca[2] en Inglaterra. Existen dos tipos de bancos: los mercantiles[3] y los comerciales. Los primeros son muy numerosos y, en general, negocian con las empresas. En los segundos van incluidos los cuatro grupos[4] principales: Lloyds, National Westminster, Barclays, y el Midland.

El folleto adjunto le informará más detalladamente, incluso[5] sobre la banca escocesa. Nuestra oficina se dedica, en particular, a las quejas relacionadas con los bancos.

Le advertimos que Correos también tiene a la disposición de los clientes servicio[6] bancario y de transferencia.

Le saluda atentamente

C. D. Prettyman (Srta)
De parte del Defensor

Anexo

1 'PO Box'; used mainly, as the name implies, for air mail.
2 'The banking system'.
3 Also *banco de negocios*.
4 *Grupo*: group of banks; also applicable to individual banks.
5 'Even' ('including').
6 Note lack of article before *servicio*.

78 Enquiry about post office banking facilities

2 February 199-

La Poste Centrale
Place Général De Gaulle
16000 Angoulême
France

Dear Sirs

I am intending to open a second business in Angoulême and would like to enquire what services you offer to small businesses.

I have in mind giro banking, and I was wondering if you could tell me how your post office bank accounts work. Secondly, is it to you that I should apply to have a telephone? And finally, do you have special rates for business mail?

I would be most grateful for any information you can send me.

Yours faithfully

Mostyn Evans
Proprietor

78 Correos: solicitando información sobre operaciones bancarias

Servicio de Correos
Plaza 23 de Febrero
Marbella
España.

2 de febrero de 199-

Señores:

Tengo el propósito de abrir un segundo negocio en Marbella y quisiera me enviaran información sobre los servicios que ustedes ofrecen a la[1] pequeña empresa.

Tengo pensado efectuar operaciones bancarias por giro postal,[2] y me pregunto si pudieran proporcionarme información sobre los tipos de cuentas que ustedes ofrecen. En segundo lugar, ¿es a ustedes a quienes[3] debo de solicitar la instalación de un teléfono? Y por último, ¿disponen de tarifas especiales para la correspondencia de empresas?[4]

Les agradecería cualquier información que pudieran enviarme, y les saludo cordialmente.

Mostyn Evans
Propietario

1 A standard way of referring to the whole sector.
2 Specifically: 'by money order'.
3 Rather involved syntax: 'Is it to you to whom ...?'.
4 Alternatives: *correspondencia comercial* or *empresarial* (though *comercial* obviously has broader meaning).

79 Enquiry about opening a post office account

8 March 199-

Bureau Central
Postes et Télécommunications
Paris
France

Dear Sirs

I do not know exactly who to address this letter to and hope that it will reach the right service.

I wish to obtain information about opening a Post Office account, to enable my French customers to settle my invoices in France and permit me to pay certain of my French suppliers by cheque.

Would you please be kind enough to inform me of your formalities and send me the necessary forms?

Yours faithfully

Eric Clifford
Managing Director

79 Solicitando información sobre apertura de cuenta por giro postal

Bureau Central
Postes et Télécommunications
París
Francia.

8 de marzo de 199-

Distinguidos señores:

No sé exactamente a quien dirigirme con la presente, aunque[1] espero que llegue al servicio apropiado.

Deseo obtener información sobre cómo abrir una cuenta en Correos, con objeto de que mis clientes franceses salden[2] mis facturas en Francia y que yo pueda abonar con cheque a varios de mis abastecedores de dicho país.

Tengan la amabilidad[3] de enviarme información sobre los trámites a seguir, junto con la solicitud necesaria para abrir dicha cuenta.

Atentamente les saluda,

Julián Bakero
Director Gerente

1 'Although'.
2 Subjunctive after *con objeto de que*; note that *pueda* is also governed by the same phrase.
3 *Tener la amabilidad de*: 'be so kind as to'.

80 Opening poste restante

18 April 199-

La Poste Centrale
Place Bellecour
69001 Lyon
France

Gentlemen

We are in the process of moving our French subsidiary from Villeurbanne to Saint Priest; the move should be completed some time in the next month.

Could we ask you on receipt of this letter and, until further notice, to retain all mail addressed to us poste restante at your central office?

Please inform us if there are any other formalities to observe. Enclosed is an addressed envelope and international reply coupon for your reply.

Thank you in advance.

Arthur T Goldberg
On behalf of Software Supplies Inc.

Encs

80 Retención de correspondencia en lista

El Director
Servicio de Correos
Gran Vía, 3
Valladolid
España.   18 de abril de 199-

Estimado Señor:

Estamos en vías de trasladar nuestra filial española de
Valladolid a Salamanca, traslado[1] que se efectuará durante el mes próximo.

Les agradeceríamos que cuando reciban esta carta, y hasta próximo aviso,[2]
retengan[3] en su oficina central todo el correo dirigido a nuestro nombre.

Sírvanse también informarnos sobre si debemos cumplir algún otro requisito.[4]
Adjunto les remitimos sobre con nuestro nombre y dirección[5] y cupón
internacional de respuesta para que nos den contestación.

Dándoles[6] las gracias anticipadas, les saludamos atentamente,

Arthur T. Goldberg
De parte de Software Suppliers Inc.

Anexos

1   No article as '*traslado*' is held to be in apposition to previous information.
2   Literally, 'until next warning'.
3   The subjunctive here, after *agradeceríamos*, acquires the force of a polite request.
4   'Requirement', 'prerequisite'.
5   Alternative: *domicilio*.
6   A present participle/gerund, typically used to round off a letter (cf. 'thanking you',
    'requesting you', 'reminding you' . . .).